W9-BTS-625

Better Homes and Gardens®

CHRISTMAS ORNAMENTS

WE CARE!

The Crafts Department at Better Homes and Gardens® Books assembled this collection of
projects for your crafting pleasure. Our staff is committed to providing you with clear
and concise instructions so that you can complete each project. We guarantee your satisfaction
with this book for as long as you own it. We welcome your comments and suggestions.
Please address your correspondence to Better Homes and Gardens® Books Crafts Department,
1716 Locust Street, LS-352X, Des Moines, IA 50336.

©Copyright 1991 by Meredith Corporation, Des Moines, Iowa.
All Rights Reserved. Printed in the United States of America.
First Edition. Printing Number and Year: 5 4   96 95 94 93
Library of Congress Catalog Card Number: 90-64099
ISBN: 0-696-01922-1 (hard cover)
ISBN: 0-696-01923-X (trade paperback)

BETTER HOMES AND GARDENS® BOOKS

Vice President, Editorial Director: Elizabeth P. Rice
Art Director: Ernest Shelton
Managing Editor: David A. Kirchner
Project Editor: Marsha Jahns
Project Managers: Liz Anderson,
    Jennifer Speer Ramundt

Crafts Editor: Sara Jane Treinen
Senior Crafts Editors: Beverly Rivers, Patricia Wilens
Associate Crafts Editor: Nancy Reames

Associate Art Directors: Neoma Thomas,
    Linda Ford Vermie, Randall Yontz
Assistant Art Directors: Lynda Haupert,
    Harijs Priekulis, Tom Wegner
Graphic Designers: Mary Schlueter Bendgen,
    Michael Burns
Art Production: Director, John Berg;
    Associate, Joe Heuer;
    Office Manager, Michaela Lester

President, Book Group: James F. Stack
Vice President, Retail Marketing: Jamie L. Martin
Vice President, Administrative Services: Rick Rundall

BETTER HOMES AND GARDENS® MAGAZINE
President, Magazine Group: James A. Autry
Editorial Director: Doris Eby

MEREDITH CORPORATION OFFICERS
Chairman of the Executive Committee: E. T. Meredith III
Chairman of the Board: Robert A. Burnett
President and Chief Executive Officer: Jack D. Rehm

Christmas Ornaments
Editor: Nancy Reames
Graphic Designer: Harijs Priekulis
Editorial Project Manager: Liz Anderson
Publishing Systems Text Processor: Paula Forest
Contributing Writer: Mary Jean Jecklin
Contributing Illustrator: Chris Neubauer

Cover project: See pages 24 and 25.

CONTENTS

An Americana Collection
A Star-Spangled Hurrah

This spirited collection of red, white, and blue ornaments pays tribute to the symbols of our national heritage. Here are six painted wooden American folk-art ornaments, a stitched and stuffed patriotic elephant and donkey, red-and-white candy wreaths, and antiqued-tin liberty bells.

Graceful Adornments
An Elegant Celebration

Create a treasure trove of luscious ornaments for your Victorian or refined country-style tree with the assortment of paper, lace, and flowery ornaments in this chapter. A distinctive beaded and tatted covering graces a clear glass globe and a gentle cut-paper angel, trimmed in gold, presides over an evergreen wreath. A delicately smocked ivory ball will become a beautiful pomander when it's sprayed with a spicy scent.

Holiday Critters
A Woodland Carnival

Animal lovers will love these whimsical ornaments. The cross-stitched foursome, engaged in winter sports, are charmers whether they're placed atop a tree or trimming a Christmas package. Here also are dough bear ornaments that, like the cross-stitched animals, are actively pursuing their favorite pastimes.

Fun and Easy Ornaments
For Friends and Family

Create ornaments for special friends and family. For a new baby, there are three cut-paper animal ornaments that can commemorate baby's first Christmas. Toddlers will enjoy hanging the easy-bake "clay" figurines year after year. Make and send the four Christmas cards to your friends; they'll get a surprise pop-up ornament heralding your wishes to them.

Handcrafted with Love
A Country Sampling

For a heartwarming country Christmas, choose from this collection of ornaments. Make the puffed heart ornaments from your old sweaters and odd buttons, or stitch the cross-stitch quilt designs that are assembled into soft "quilt pillows." For discriminating Santa collectors, we've assembled a grouping of Santa ornaments.

Acknowledgments

AN AMERICANA COLLECTION

A STAR-SPANGLED HURRAH

For a spirited Christmas, create an all-American tree decorated with our country's most renowned symbols of freedom. All carefully crafted, these patriotic ornaments say they were made in America with love. Best of all, these favorites can be used to commemorate the Fourth of July or to show off your patriotic spirit year-round.

The easy-to-make gold felt antiqued stars, *right,* are inspired by Old Glory and the star of the East that led the wise men to the stable in Bethlehem. Joined together with rough twine that's threaded with cranberry red beads, the stars add holiday sparkle to your tree. Instructions for this golden garland are on page 10.

The other ornaments shown at *right* are described more fully on pages 6–9. Included are wooden Uncle Sams in smart striped top hats and trousers, frizzy-haired Lady Liberties decked out in diadems and banners, bald eagles perched pridefully on shields, Uncle Sam top hats, stick-handled flags, and flaglike heart ornaments.

From other crafting materials, there are weathered-tin Liberty Bells, red-and-white-striped candy wreaths, and fabric-stuffed elephant, donkey, and cat pull toys.

Pull toys have amused American youngsters since our country's earliest days. These delightful partisan donkey and elephant pull toys, *above,* roll along on red and blue star buttons, attended by an apolitical pussycat.

The elephant and donkey show their colors in fabric splashed with tiny stars. The neutral muslin cat, sporting a saucy red bow and a hat that resembles caps worn by early patriots, deftly holds a diminutive American flag in its curled tail.

For the moment all three animals have forgotten about creating political fireworks—except for the sparks of joy that light up the faces of the lucky recipients of these fanciful packages. Get out all three ornaments again to display on Election Day.

Instructions for these three ornaments begin on page 10.

Your patriotism will ring out loud and clear when you add these replicas of the famous Liberty Bell—crack and all—to your holiday wreath or tree. The bells are made of tin, a metal commonly used in colonial America, and topped with cheery red grosgrain bows. Their weathered appearance evokes a feeling of nostalgia for the historic era that produced the cast-iron original.

Our instructions call for old tin but we also give instructions for weathering new tin.

Instructions for the Liberty Bell ornament are on page 13.

Y ou'll have a razzle-dazzle Christmas when the Uncle Sam and Lady Liberty wooden ornaments, *opposite,* attended by other patriotic embellishments, preside over your holiday festivities.

Other ornaments include a wooden American flag on a small stick and a bald eagle that has twigs for feet. Wired stars burst from the red-white-and-blue heart ornament like firecrackers. There's also a large version of Uncle Sam's

hat. All of the ornaments are painted with acrylics, lightly sanded, and antiqued.

Melt red-and-white candies in muffin tins to make the candy wreaths, *above.* Use other types of hard Christmas candy to make other versions of

this wreath. Spray polyurethane over the finished wreaths and they will last for many Christmases.

Instructions for the wooden ornaments are on pages 13–17. See page 10 to make the candy wreaths.

Candy Wreath

Shown on pages 4, 5, and 9.

Wreath measures 3½ inches in diameter.

MATERIALS
For one ornament
Six red-and-white hard peppermint candies
6 inches of ¼-inch-wide red grosgrain ribbon
3½-inch-diameter tart pan
Clear polyurethane spray
White crafts glue
8-inch strand of gold metallic thread for the hanger; awl

INSTRUCTIONS
Preheat the oven to 325 degrees. Remove paper wrapping from hard candies. Arrange the six candies flat-side down in a circle around the bottom of the tart pan.

Bake for 4 to 5 minutes, or until the individual candies begin to melt together. If the wreath cooks too long, the center will close. Remove pan from the oven and use the awl to poke a hole for hanging along the edge of the wreath. Place the pan in the freezer for a few minutes to cool.

After the wreath has cooled, invert the pan and remove the wreath by applying pressure to the back of the pan with both thumbs.

Spray one side of the wreath with polyurethane; allow to dry. Spray the other side; dry.

Tie a ribbon bow; use glue to attach the ribbon to the wreath below the hanging hole. Thread the hole with an 8-inch piece of gold thread. Tie the thread into a loop.

Star Garland

Shown on pages 4 and 5.

Garland measures approximately 13 feet long.

MATERIALS
Nine pieces of 9x12-inch yellow felt
Matching sewing thread
Raw umber acrylic paint for antiquing the stars
Tracing paper; paper plate
30 red ½-inch-diameter wooden beads; 16 feet of narrow twine
Fiberfill
Measuring tape

INSTRUCTIONS
Fold tracing paper in half; lay fold of paper on dashed line of full-size star pattern, *left*, and trace star. Cut out pattern, completing star shape.

Fold a felt piece in half and place completed star pattern on top; draw around star pattern. Cutting through both layers of felt, cut out two stars. Repeat for all nine felt pieces, making a total of 18 stars.

Make an overhand knot 5¼ inches from one end of the twine. Thread a red bead onto the twine from the other end; push the bead up to the knot and tie another overhand knot to secure the bead. Continue adding beads and tying knots directly after one another until there are a total of three beads and four knots. Measure 5¼ inches from the last knot, then place the twine between two star pieces; match points and pin stars together. Using a ⅛-inch seam allowance, machine stitch around the star edge through the twine. Measure 5¼ inches from the star and make an overhand knot; add beads and knots as before. Continue adding stars, placing three beads and four knots between them until nine stars are in place. Add one more set of three beads and four knots following the last star.

Carefully slit the back of one star in each sewn pair; lightly stuff the star and hand-sew the slit closed.

To antique the stars, place a small amount of raw umber paint on the paper plate. Dab a scrap of felt in the paint and blot excess paint until scrap is nearly dry. Using the felt scrap, rub paint lightly over both sides of the stars, adding more paint to the felt scrap as needed.

Patriotic Cat Ornament

Shown on pages 4–6.

Cat measures approximately 3¾ inches high.

MATERIALS
For one ornament
5x10-inch piece of muslin for the cat body
Small scrap of red-white-and-blue fabric for the hat
Toothpick with a tiny paper flag on one end
One ceramic star button
8 inches of ⅜-inch red satin ribbon
Tracing paper
Fiberfill
Black permanent marker to draw facial features
9 inches of gold metallic thread for the hanger
White crafts glue or hot-glue gun

INSTRUCTIONS
Trace full-size cat pattern, *opposite*, onto tracing paper and cut

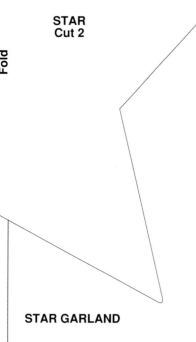

Fold

**STAR
Cut 2**

STAR GARLAND

out paper pattern. Fold muslin in half widthwise with right sides facing; place cat pattern on top and draw around pattern. The marked lines are stitching lines.

Sew the two body pieces together, leaving an opening as indicated on pattern. Cut out cat, allowing for ⅛-inch seams. Clip curves and turn right side out. Stuff firmly; whip-stitch the opening closed.

Cut a 2x2¾-inch rectangle from the red-white-and-blue fabric scrap for the hat. Fold rectangle in half widthwise so the wrong sides are together.

Referring to the illustrations *below, right,* fold corners down to meet at center. Add a little glue under each of these folds or take a stitch or two to hold the shape. With a finger inserted into the center opening of the hat, fold a flap up on each side of the hat. Add a little glue or take a stitch to hold the flaps up. Glue the hat over the cat's ear.

Tie the red ribbon into a bow around the cat's neck and sew the button to the center of the bow.

Tack toothpick with flag to tail. Draw facial features on the head with permanent marker.

Sew gold thread to center of back for the hanger; tie into loop.

Elephant Pull Toy Ornament

Shown on pages 4–6.

Elephant measures approximately 3½ inches high.

MATERIALS
For one ornament
5x10-inch piece of navy-and-white star fabric for the body and ears

Scrap of red-and-white stripe fabric for the blanket

Red and navy embroidery floss for the mouth and tail

Two tiny white buttons for eyes

Four ceramic star-shape buttons for wheels

Fiberfill; tracing paper

Pinking shears to cut blanket

9 inches of gold metallic thread

INSTRUCTIONS
Trace the full-size elephant and ear patterns on page 12 onto tracing paper; cut out patterns.

With right sides facing, fold navy-and-white body fabric in half widthwise. Position elephant pattern on fabric; draw around pattern. Position and draw around ear pattern twice. Sew around body and two ears on drawn line, leaving openings for turning as marked on patterns.

Cut out body and ear pieces allowing for ⅛-inch seam allowances. Clip body curves; turn right side out and stuff firmly. Whip-stitch opening closed. Clip ear curves; turn each right side out and stuff lightly. Fold under open edges of ears and press. Whip-stitch ears to sides of elephant's head as indicated on pattern, catching both layers of ear openings as you sew.

Using pinking shears, cut out a 1⅜x2¾-inch rectangle from the red-and-white stripe fabric for the blanket. Tack blanket corners to the elephant's back using the dashed line for placement.

For the tail, cut and sew six 12-inch strands of navy floss through the X, where shown on the pattern. Leave half of the floss on each side of the seam and tie an overhand knot next to the fabric. Braid floss strands for 1½ inches; tie an overhand knot at the end of the braid. Cut end of tail ½ inch beyond knot.

continued

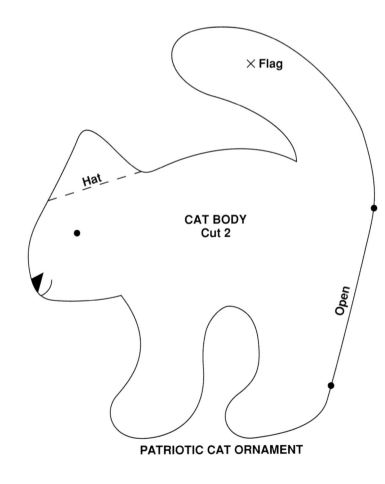

CAT BODY
Cut 2

× **Flag**

Hat

PATRIOTIC CAT ORNAMENT

Open

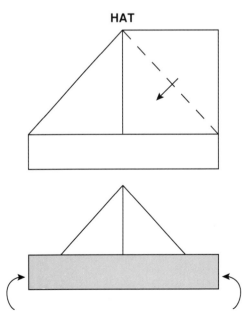

HAT

11

Sew two tiny white buttons for eyes to X on both sides of the face. Using red floss, straight stitch a mouth at the dashed line below the trunk.

For wheels, sew one star button to both sides of elephant's feet at each X.

Sew gold metallic thread to top of the back for a hanger; tie into a loop.

Donkey Pull Toy Ornament

Shown on pages 4–6.

Donkey measures approximately 4 inches high.

MATERIALS
For one ornament
5x10-inch piece of red-and-white star fabric for body
Scrap of blue-and-white star fabric for blanket
Scrap of tan felt for ears
1 yard of gray 1-ply worsted wool yarn for mane and tail
Red embroidery floss for mouth
Two tiny white buttons for eyes
Four ceramic star-shape buttons for wheels
Tracing paper
Pinking shears to cut blanket
Fiberfill
9 inches of gold metallic thread for hanger

INSTRUCTIONS
Trace full-size donkey and ear patterns, *right,* onto tracing paper; cut out patterns.

Fold red-and-white body fabric in half widthwise with right sides facing. Position donkey on fabric; draw around the pattern. Sew around body on drawn line, leaving the opening for turning as marked. Cut out donkey allowing for a ⅛-inch seam allowance. Clip the curves and turn right side out; stuff firmly and whipstitch opening closed.

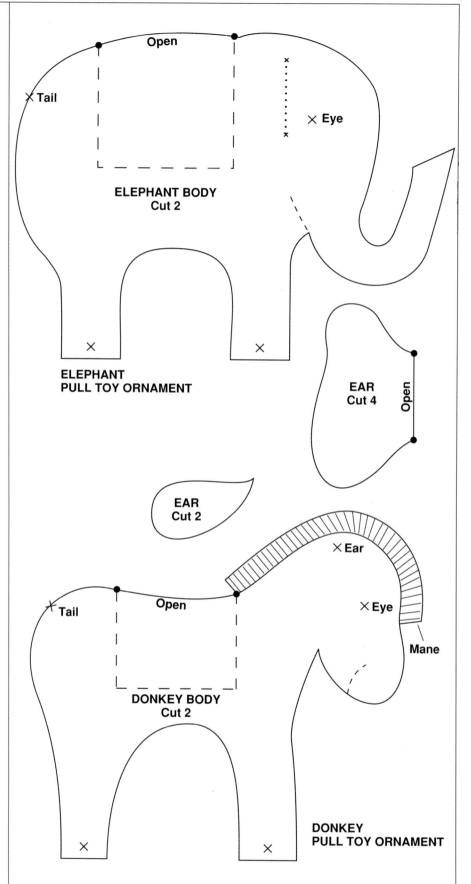

ELEPHANT BODY
Cut 2

ELEPHANT
PULL TOY ORNAMENT

× Tail
Open
× Eye

EAR
Cut 4
Open

EAR
Cut 2

DONKEY BODY
Cut 2

× Tail
Open
× Ear
× Eye
Mane

DONKEY
PULL TOY ORNAMENT

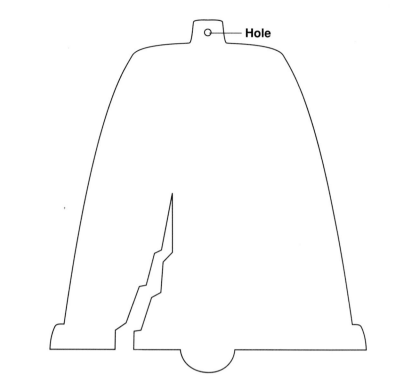

○ — Hole

TIN LIBERTY BELL

Draw two ear patterns on felt; cut out ears. Fold rounded end of ears in half and tack to X on both sides of head, pointing the fold toward the back of the donkey.

Using pinking shears cut a 1¼x2⅛-inch rectangle from the blue-and-white star fabric for the blanket. Tack the blanket corners to donkey's back using the dashed line for placement.

For the mane, loop gray wool yarn, sewing it to the head and neck of the donkey as you make each small loop. Cut mane loops open; trim evenly. Tack a 2½-inch piece of gray wool yarn to the X for the tail.

Sew two tiny white buttons to the X on both sides of the face for eyes. Using red floss, straight stitch a mouth at the dashed line on the face.

For wheels, sew one star button to both sides of donkey's feet at each X.

Sew gold metallic thread to the back for hanger; tie into a loop.

Tin Liberty-Bell Ornament

Shown on pages 4, 5, and 7.

Bell measures approximately 3¾ inches high.

MATERIALS
For one ornament
3½x4-inch piece of weathered tin
8-inch length of ¼-inch-wide red grosgrain ribbon
8-inch-long piece of red perle cotton for hanger
Tracing paper
Permanent black marker
Small tin snips
Hammer; nail; file
White crafts glue
Clear polyurethane spray

INSTRUCTIONS
Note: If you can't find weathered tin you can use new tin. Apply muriatic acid to remove the galvanizing; rinse off and leave outside to weather until the tin has the look you want for your bell.

Trace the full-size bell pattern, *above,* onto tracing paper; cut out the paper pattern. Use the perma-

nent marker to draw around the pattern atop the tin.

Using tin snips cut out the bell on marked lines. File any rough edges. Use the nail to punch a hole at the top of the bell.

Hammer bell flat. Spray with polyurethane; allow to dry.

Tie a ribbon bow; glue bow below the nail hole. Thread perle cotton through the hole; tie an overhand knot directly above the hole and then tie into a loop.

Eagle Ornament

Shown on pages 4, 5, and 8.

Eagle measures 3½ inches high.

MATERIALS
For one ornament
4-inch-square piece of ½-inch pine for eagle
2-inch-square piece of ⅛-inch birch plywood for shield
Two small branched twigs for feet
7-inch piece of ecru perle cotton for hanger
Acrylic paints in the following colors: navy blue, dark red, yellow ocher, black, and white
Assortment of small paintbrushes
Water-base antiquing medium
Matte varnish spray
Sandpaper; tracing paper
Band saw; drill; ⅛- and ³/₁₆-inch drill bits
White crafts glue

INSTRUCTIONS
Trace the full-size eagle and shield patterns on page 14 onto tracing paper. Transfer eagle pattern to ½-inch pine and shield pattern to ⅛-inch plywood; cut shapes from wood.

Drill a ⅛-inch-wide hole ¼ inch deep in the top of the eagle's head for the hanger. Sand all pieces.

Paint the pieces as indicated on the patterns. Lightly sand again for an antique look. Brush antiquing medium over the pieces; let dry about 5 minutes and wipe off excess. Glue shield to the center of the eagle's chest.

continued

Drill a 3/16-inch-wide hole ¼ inch deep in the bottom of each leg to accept the twig feet. Trim the branched twigs down to look like feet. Paint the twigs with yellow ocher paint. After paint has dried, shape ends as necessary; glue into holes.

Spray with matte varnish. Add glue to hole in top of head; push both ends of perle cotton into hole to form a loop.

Flag Ornament

Shown on pages 4, 5, and 8.

Flag measures approximately 8½ inches high.

MATERIALS
For one ornament
4x2-inch piece of ⅛-inch birch plywood for flag
2-inch-square piece of ⅜-inch birch plywood for star
7-inch twig for pole
8-inch piece of thin twine
Acrylic paints in the following colors: navy blue, dark red, yellow ocher, and white
Assortment of small paintbrushes
Water-base antiquing medium
Matte varnish spray
Sandpaper; tracing paper
Band saw; drill; ⅛- and 3/16-inch drill bits
White crafts glue

INSTRUCTIONS
Trace the full-size flag and star patterns, *right*, onto tracing paper. Transfer flag pattern to ⅛-inch plywood and star pattern to ⅜-inch plywood; cut shapes from wood. Drill two ⅛-inch holes through the flag, where shown, for attaching the flag to the pole. Drill a 3/16-inch-wide hole ¼ inch deep in the bottom of the star, where shown, to accept the twig. Sand all pieces.

Paint pieces in colors indicated on patterns. Lightly sand again for antique look. Brush antiquing medium over pieces; let dry about 5 minutes; wipe off excess.

Glue twig into the bottom of the star. Spray star and flag with matte varnish. Use twine to tie the flag onto twig below star.

14

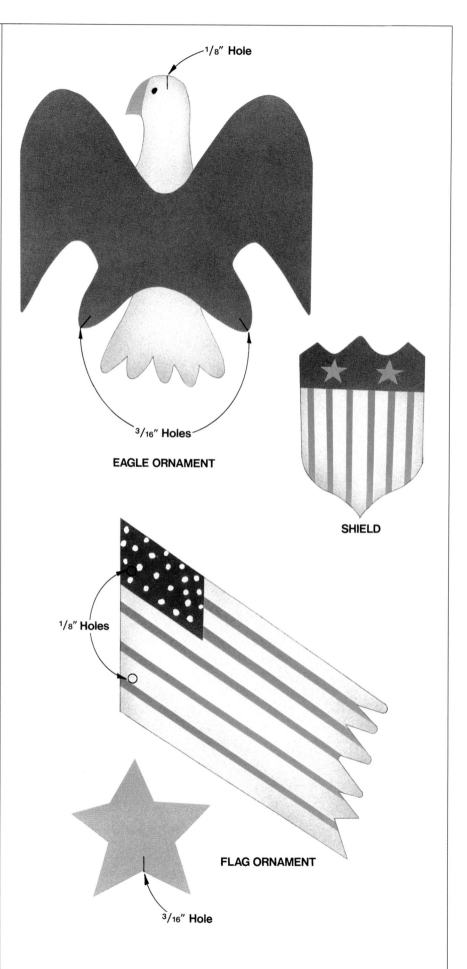

1/8″ Hole

3/16″ Holes

EAGLE ORNAMENT

SHIELD

1/8″ Holes

FLAG ORNAMENT

3/16″ Hole

Heart and Stars Ornament

Shown on pages 4, 5, and 8.

The ornament measures approximately 4 inches high.

MATERIALS
For one ornament
3-inch-square piece of 1-inch pine for heart
3-inch-square piece of ¼-inch birch plywood for stars
6-inch piece of thin wire
7-inch piece of ecru perle cotton for hanger
Acrylic paints in the following colors: navy blue, dark red, yellow ocher, and white
Assortment of small paintbrushes
Water-base antiquing medium
Matte varnish spray
Sandpaper; tracing paper
Band saw; router; drill; ⅛-, 1/16-, and 3/32-inch drill bits
White crafts glue

INSTRUCTIONS
Trace the full-size heart and star patterns, *above, right,* onto tracing paper. Transfer one heart pattern to 1-inch pine and three stars to ¼-inch plywood; cut pieces from wood.

Using the router, cut away all edges of the heart. Referring to the patterns, drill a ⅛-inch-wide hole ¼ inch deep at the top of the left side of the heart. Drill a 3/32-inch-wide hole ¼ inch deep in the upper left side of the front of the heart. Drill a 1/16-inch-wide hole ¼ inch deep in the bottom of all three stars. Sand all pieces.

Paint the pieces in colors indicated on the patterns. Lightly sand again for an antique look. Brush antiquing medium over the pieces; let dry about 5 minutes; wipe off excess. Spray pieces with matte varnish.

Cut wire into three pieces of varying lengths. Glue one end of each piece into the bottom of each star. Glue the other ends of the three wires into the 3/32-inch hole in the upper left side of the front of the heart. Add glue to the hole in the top of the heart; push both ends of perle cotton into the hole to form a loop.

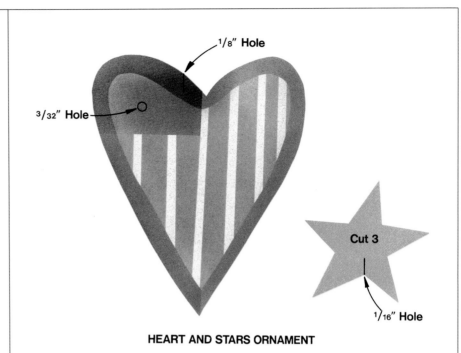

HEART AND STARS ORNAMENT

Lady Liberty Ornament

Shown on pages 4, 5, and 8.

The ornament measures approximately 6 inches high.

MATERIALS
For one ornament
5-inch length of 1-inch-diameter wood dowel for body
3-inch square of ⅛-inch birch plywood for crown and arms
9x1½-inch piece of red-and-white-stripe fabric for sash
Gold embroidery floss
Small piece of clean raw wool for hair; brown fabric dye
7-inch piece of ecru perle cotton for hanger
Acrylic paints in the following colors: navy blue, dark red, black, white, and flesh
Assortment of small paintbrushes
Water-base antiquing medium
Matte varnish spray; small brads
Sandpaper; tracing paper
Band saw; drill; ⅛-inch drill bit
White crafts glue; hot-glue gun

INSTRUCTIONS
Trace the full-size crown and arm patterns on page 16 onto tracing paper. Transfer the patterns to ⅛-inch plywood; cut pieces from wood. Drill a ⅛-inch-wide hole ¼ inch deep in the center of one end of dowel for hanger. Sand pieces.

Dye wool for the hair with a small amount of brown dye; allow wool to dry.

Paint the pieces in colors indicated on the patterns. Lightly sand again for an antique look. Brush the antiquing medium over the pieces; let dry about 5 minutes; wipe off excess.

Nail crown to back of head using two brads; nail the arms to the sides of the body. Spray the ornament with matte varnish. Add crafts glue to the hole in the top of dowel; push both ends of perle cotton into hole.

For the hair, glue the dyed wool around top and sides of head with crafts glue.

For the sash, fold fabric in thirds lengthwise to make a 9x½-inch strip. Beginning at the right shoulder edge, hot-glue the fabric diagonally down across the body front and up across the back, leaving about 1½ inches of the end of the fabric unglued. Wrap and knot gold embroidery floss around the fabric where it hits the shoulder; hot-glue or nail the knot at the shoulder. Unfold the 1½-inch tail of the fabric.

15

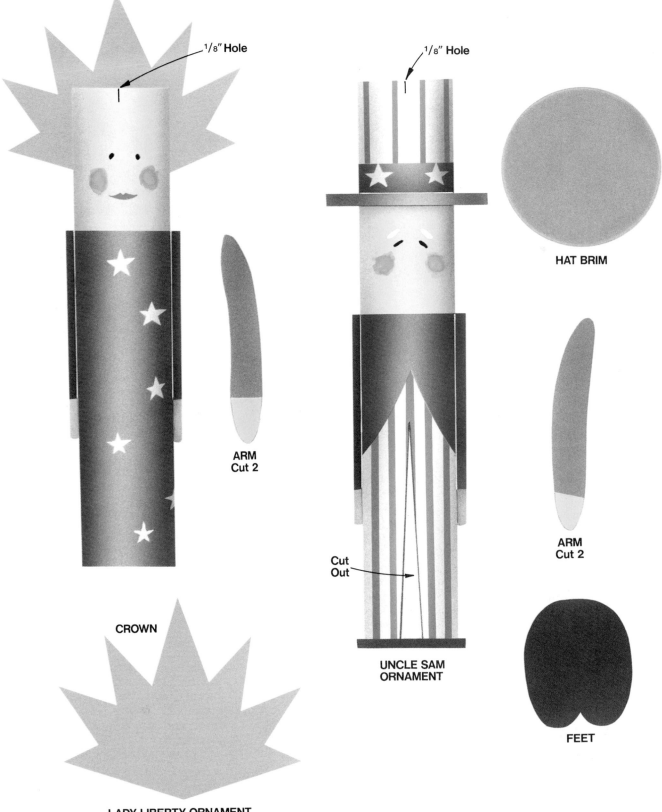

¹/₈″ **Hole**

¹/₈″ **Hole**

HAT BRIM

ARM
Cut 2

ARM
Cut 2

CROWN

Cut
Out

UNCLE SAM
ORNAMENT

FEET

LADY LIBERTY ORNAMENT

Uncle Sam Ornament

Shown on pages 4, 5, and 8.

Uncle Sam measures approximately 6 inches high.

MATERIALS
For one ornament
6-inch piece of 1-inch-diameter wood dowel for body and hat

3-inch-square piece of ⅛-inch birch plywood for arms, feet, and hat brim

½-inch piece of ⅛-inch-diameter wood dowel to join hat to head

Small piece of clean raw wool for hair and beard

7-inch piece of ecru perle cotton for hanger

Acrylic paints in the following colors: navy blue, dark red, black, white, and flesh

Assortment of small paintbrushes

Water-base antiquing medium

Matte varnish spray

Sandpaper; tracing paper

Band saw; drill; ⅛-inch drill bit

Small brads; white crafts glue

INSTRUCTIONS
Trace the full-size hat brim, feet, and arm patterns, *opposite,* onto tracing paper. Transfer patterns to ⅛-inch plywood; cut pieces from wood. Cut a 1⅛-inch piece of dowel off one end of the 6-inch-long dowel for the hat. Cut a 2½-inch-long tapered slice in the center of the other end of the dowel for the legs. Sand all pieces.

Paint the pieces in colors indicated on the patterns. Lightly sand again for an antique look. Brush antiquing medium over the pieces; let dry about 5 minutes; wipe off excess.

Nail the hat brim to the bottom of the hat with two brads set off center. Drill ⅛-inch-wide holes ¼-inch deep in the center of the hat brim and in the center of the flat edge of the head dowel. Add a small amount of glue to the two holes and insert the ⅛-inch-diameter dowel piece into the holes to join the hat to the head. Drill a ⅛-inch-wide hole ¼ inch deep in center top of hat for the hanger.

Nail the feet to the bottom of the legs; nail the arms to both sides of the body at the shoulders.

Spray with matte varnish. Add glue to hole in top of head; push both ends of perle cotton into hole. Glue a small amount of wool to the back of the head for the hair; glue another piece of wool to the face for the beard.

Top Hat Ornament

Shown on pages 4, 5, and 8.

Hat measures approximately 2 inches high.

MATERIALS
For one ornament
1¾-inch piece of 1¼-diameter wood dowel for top of hat

3-inch square of ¼-inch birch plywood for brim and star

¾-inch piece of ⅛-inch-diameter wood dowel

6-inch-long piece of ecru perle cotton for hanger

Acrylic paints in the following colors: navy blue, dark red, yellow ocher, and white

Assortment of small paintbrushes

Water-base antiquing medium

Matte varnish spray

Sandpaper; tracing paper

Band saw; drill; ⅛-inch drill bit

Small brads; white crafts glue

INSTRUCTIONS
Trace the full-size hat brim and star patterns, *right,* onto tracing paper. Transfer patterns to ¼-inch plywood; cut pieces from wood. Sand all pieces.

Drill a ⅛-inch-wide hole ¼ inch deep in the center top of the larger dowel for the hanger. Drill a ⅛-inch-wide hole ¼ inch deep in the bottom of the star and into the brim of the hat where marked, being careful not to go through the brim.

Paint the pieces in colors indicated on the patterns. Sand again lightly for an antique look. Brush antiquing medium over the pieces; let dry about 5 minutes; wipe off excess.

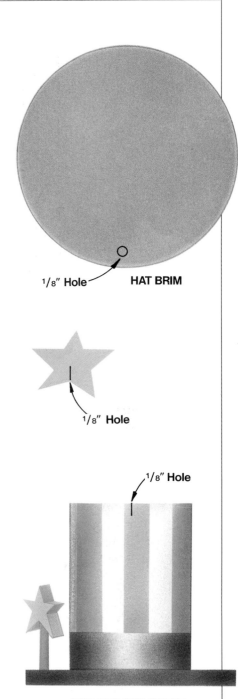

⅛" Hole   **HAT BRIM**

⅛" Hole

⅛" Hole

TOP HAT ORNAMENT

Glue small dowel into star and brim. Center and nail top of hat to brim with small brads.

Spray with matte varnish. Glue both ends of perle cotton into hole in the top of the hat to form a loop for the hanger.

GRACEFUL ADORNMENTS

AN ELEGANT CELEBRATION

The Victorian home at Christmas—rich with romantic handmade lace, tatted and crocheted fineries, frilly pomanders, exquisite cut-paper ornaments, and swags of flowers—mesmerizes those who yearn for the elegance of that long-ago, bygone era.

The demure hearts and heavenly host of angels adorning and topping this Christmas tree, *left* and *below,* reflect Victorian ladies' love of fine lace and flowers. All of these ornaments are made from tea-dyed muslin, lace trims, tiny pearls, and satin ribbons.

Instructions for the tree topper and heart and angel ornaments are on pages 26–29.

Thank Queen Victoria's German husband, Prince Albert, for popularizing the custom of bringing an evergreen tree into the home at Christmas.

The crocheted basket, fan, and hat, *above,* would have looked nice amid the fruits, nuts, and sweets that graced Victoria and Albert's own tree. Yet it wasn't until the early 19th century that people began using ornaments other than food.

The fold-and-cut three-dimensional paper star, *right,* is a welcome addition to any tree.

The English love of gardening is remembered *opposite* with miniature topiary trees, enchantingly lucky birds' nests, and floral heart wreaths and bow ornaments.

Instructions for the star are on page 27. The floral ornaments are on pages 29 and 30. The crocheted ornaments are on pages 32 and 33.

The frothy smocked balls, *above,* are enriched with tiny seed pearls and embellished with delicate green and pink pastel ribbons.

The shimmering glass globes nestled in the greens, *above,* have a crown of tatting and sparkling seed beads.

The balls, *opposite,* are completely covered with rich satin, plush velvet, or beautiful brocade fabrics, then topped with elegant gold braid trim.

Instructions for the smocked balls are on pages 30 and 31. The tatted ball covers and the fabric-covered balls are on pages 33–35.

All-white filigree confections made of paper or fine cotton will give a Victorian feel to any evergreen branch or wreath.

Making the pierced-paper flowers or cut-paper angel, *left,* takes a steady hand, a keen eye, and few materials other than sharp scissors.

As in nature, no two of our three tatted snowflakes, *left,* are the same. Our designs are for four-, five-, and six-pointed snowflakes.

In the 19th century, Santa Claus came to be portrayed in words and pictures as the jolly, old elf described in Clement Moore's famous poem, "A Visit From St. Nicholas." Like the papa in the poem, you, too, will laugh in spite of yourself when making the quintessential Victorian Santa ornament, *below.* Arrayed in burgundy velvet and a plush fake-fur robe, the Santa makes a festive gift decoration as well as tree ornament.

Instructions for the ornaments on the wreath, *left,* are on pages 35–38. See page 39 to make the Santa ornament.

Treetop Angel

Shown on page 19.

Angel is 25 inches long.

MATERIAL
¾ yard of muslin for body and dress

2½ yards of 3¾-inch-wide ivory lace

9½x23-inch piece of ivory tulle for wings

Polyester fiberfill

Four burgundy ribbon roses

½-yard string of pearls

1½ yards of 3/16-inch-wide burgundy satin ribbon with picot edge

Tiny gold heart charm

3 yards of ⅛-inch-wide dark green satin ribbon

⅓ yard of 1/16-inch-wide dark green satin ribbon

Brown and rose embroidery floss for eyes and mouth

One skein of Size 3 brown perle cotton for hair; brown sewing thread to match perle cotton

Tracing paper

Tea bags for dyeing fabrics

White crafts glue

INSTRUCTIONS
Note: Patterns include ¼-inch seam allowances. Sew all pieces with right sides together.

Use hot water and tea bags to make a strong tea solution. Soak muslin, lace, and tulle in tea solution for about 30 minutes. Dry and press muslin.

Trace the patterns for body, bodice, and arms, *right,* onto the tracing paper.

CUTTING: Cut a 17x36-inch piece of muslin for the skirt. Fold the remaining 10-inch-wide piece of muslin in half widthwise. Place patterns on fabric fold and cut out pieces. Cut two body pieces, two bodices, and four arm pieces.

SEWING: Transfer the facial markings to one body piece. Embroider eyes with brown floss using straight stitches. Satin-stitch lips with rose floss.

Stitch the two body sections together leaving the bottom open. Turn right side out. Stitch two arm pieces together leaving tops

26

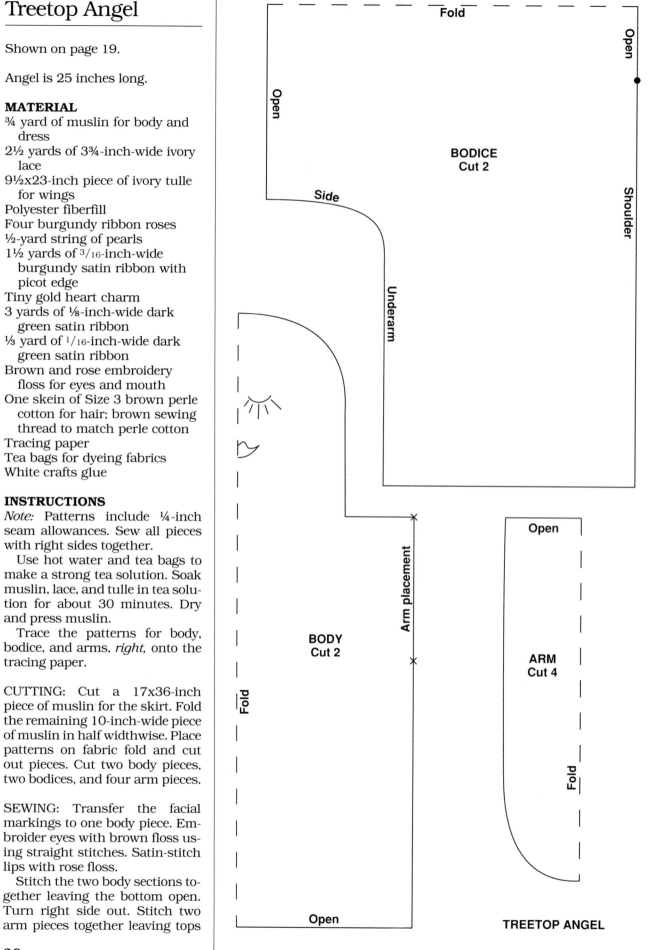

open. Repeat for other arm. Turn and stuff arms; sew openings closed. Sew arms to body along side seams. Stuff head and body; sew opening closed.

Stitch the side and underarm seams of the bodice. Stitch the shoulder seams, leaving an opening as indicated for the head.

Stitch the two short sides of the skirt together. Turn under ¼-inch for hem. Cut a 1⅔-yard length of lace for the hem of the skirt; gather lace and sew to hem. Gather top edge of skirt for waist. Stitch skirt waist to bodice waist.

Turn under raw edges of bodice at neck and sleeves. Baste edges of sleeves; place dress over body and gather the basting threads around arms. Gather remaining lace; place it around neck with opening in back. Tack in place.

FINISHING: For hair, leave twisted perle cotton in skein; tie threads around loops at each end of skein then remove paper label bands. Stitch one loop to center back of head. Stitch twisted skein to doll while wrapping the skein around head; tuck second end under skein in back of head.

Cut string of pearls into a 3-inch length and a 15-inch length. Set aside the 3-inch length. Weave the 15-inch length of pearls through the twisted skein of perle cotton on the head; tack in place.

Make a small bow from 1/16-inch dark green ribbon. Sew bow to hair; sew ribbon rose to center of bow. Make several 1-inch loops with the remaining 1/16-inch dark green ribbon; secure center of loops with thread to make a bow. Make a matching loop with remaining pearl length and secure it to the ribbon bow. Sew the bow to the top of the lace at the neckline. Sew three ribbon roses and the heart charm to center of bow.

Cut ⅛-inch-wide dark green ribbon in half. Glue the two dark green and one burgundy ribbons together around angel's waist. Tie them into a bow at the side.

For the wings, cut tulle into two 9½x11½-inch pieces. Lay pieces on top of each other; sew a gathering thread down the center of the width of the pieces. Gather; sew to top of lace at back of neckline.

Lace Heart Ornament

Shown on pages 18 and 19.

Heart is 3¾ inches across at the widest point.

MATERIALS
For one heart ornament
5x10-inch piece of muslin fabric
½ yard of 3-inch-wide ecru lace
Polyester fiberfill
15 inches of ⅛-inch-wide dark green satin ribbon
Two mauve ribbon roses
35 seed pearls
10 inches of gold metallic thread for hanger
Tracing paper
One or two tea bags for dyeing lace and muslin

INSTRUCTIONS
Make a strong tea solution using hot water and one or two tea bags. Soak lace and muslin in tea until the desired color is achieved (about 30 minutes). Allow fabric and lace to dry.

Fold tracing paper in half; place fold of paper on fold line of full-size heart design, *above, right.* Trace design and cut out pattern.

Fold muslin in half widthwise. Place pattern on top of muslin and draw around heart; cutting along the drawn line, cut out two heart shapes for each ornament.

Beginning at center top, pin wrong side of lace around right side of one heart. Overlap the lace when you come back to center top of heart; trim away excess lace. Hand-baste lace to the heart ¼ inch from outside edges.

To keep lace out of the way for machine stitching, fold lace toward the center and pin.

Pin the right side of the second (back) heart shape atop the lace side of the first (front) heart shape. Sew around the edges along the basting line. Carefully cut a 1½-inch opening in the back heart only. Turn right side out through opening and stuff; hand-sew opening closed.

Gather lace around heart; secure the center tuft of lace with thread. Tie ribbon into a double

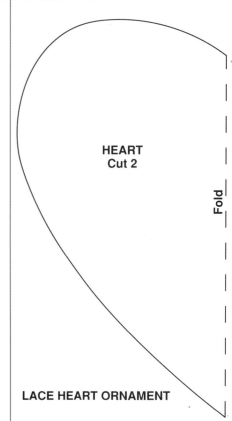

HEART
Cut 2

Fold

LACE HEART ORNAMENT

looped bow around the gathered lace tuft. String 35 pearls on thread and sew to the gathered lace next to the bow. Sew two ribbon roses to the center of the gathered lace tuft. Sew the gold metallic thread through center top of the heart and tie a loop.

Three-Dimensional Star Ornaments

Shown on page 20.

The stars measure 5¼ inches in diameter.

MATERIALS
For two ornaments
Three 8½x11-inch sheets of parchment
Tracing paper; graphite paper
Stapler; pencil
Sharp 4-inch embroidery or manicure scissors
Crafts knife
Sewing needle
Thread to match parchment
20 inches of gold metallic thread for hanger

continued

INSTRUCTIONS

Trace the full-size star pattern, *below*, onto tracing paper.

Cut the three sheets of parchment in half widthwise. Set aside three pieces of paper. Holding one set of three pieces together, fold them in half lengthwise. Use the graphite paper to transfer the pattern to the top of the folded papers, aligning the folds with the fold line on the pattern. Remove the pattern and graphite paper when tracing is complete. Staple the three sheets, outside the traced design area, to hold sheets in place while you are cutting.

To cut out the design, begin by cutting the areas closest to the fold. Proceed, cutting away the inside portions and finally cutting the outside edges.

After the design is cut, unfold the stars; do not take them apart.

Hand-sew the three stars together along the fold line. Space stitches approximately ⅛ inch apart. Open the stars and bend the six halves to form a radiating circle.

Repeat for the second star.

Cut the length of gold metallic thread in half; string thread through the top hole and tie a knot.

Little Angel Ornament

Shown on pages 18 and 19.

Angel is 5 inches high.

MATERIALS
For one ornament
9x15-inch piece of muslin for body and dress
4x10-inch piece of ivory tulle for wings
13 inches of 1½-inch-wide ivory lace for collar
One skein of Size 3 brown perle cotton for hair; brown sewing thread to match perle cotton
3-inch strand of pearls
⅓ yard of 1/16-inch-wide dark green ribbon
One burgundy ribbon rose
Brown and rose embroidery floss for eyes and mouth
Polyester fiberfill
White crafts glue or hot-glue gun; tracing paper
Tea bags for dyeing fabrics

INSTRUCTIONS
Note: Pattern includes ¼-inch seam allowances. Sew pieces with right sides together unless otherwise instructed.

Use hot water and tea bags to make a strong tea solution. Soak muslin, lace, and tulle in tea solution about 30 minutes. Allow fabrics to dry; press muslin.

Trace the pattern for the body, *top, right*, onto tracing paper.

CUTTING: For the skirt, cut a 3x9-inch piece of muslin along the selvage. Fold remaining 12x9-inch piece of muslin in half; place pattern on fold of 12x4½-inch piece of fabric and cut one body piece. Reposition pattern and cut second body piece.

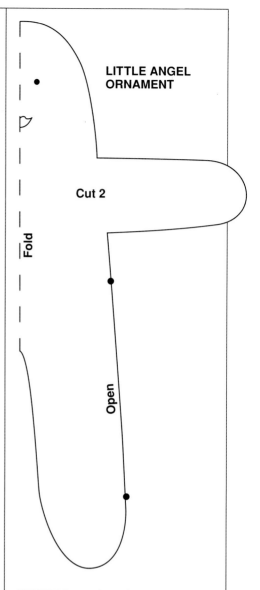

LITTLE ANGEL ORNAMENT

Cut 2

Fold

Open

SEWING: Embroider the mouth with rose floss using satin stitches; make French knots for eyes using brown floss.

Stitch two body pieces together leaving one outside leg seam open as indicated. Turn right side out; stuff and stitch opening closed.

Sew the short sides of the skirt piece together; selvage edge becomes the bottom edge. Turn under ¼ inch on raw edge; hand gather for waist band and tack skirt below arms, with seam in back. Gather one long edge of lace to fit around neck; place over head and tack in place, with seam at center back.

FINISHING: Cut one 6-inch strand of perle cotton for the hanger; knot in a loop and tack to the top of the head. Cut fourteen 5-inch strands of perle cotton for

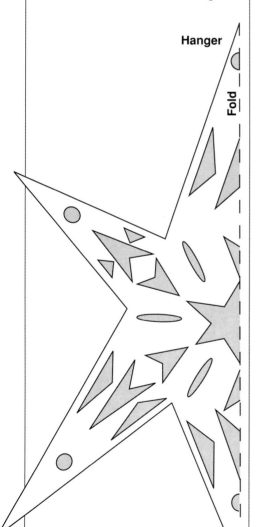

Hanger

Fold

THREE-DIMENSIONAL STAR ORNAMENT

the hair. Center the strands across the top of the head and glue or sew them in place down the center back of the head. Loop ends under at sides of head and glue or sew in place.

Cut pearl strand into two 1½-inch pieces; glue each pearl strand around hair loops for pony tails.

Cut tulle into two 4x5-inch pieces. Gather both pieces in the middle and tack them together to the center top of the back for wings.

Cut ribbon in half; make two bows and sew or glue both to center front at the neckline. Attach ribbon rose to center of bows.

Angel Bust Ornament

Shown on pages 18 and 19.

Angel measures 4½ inches high.

MATERIALS
For one ornament
6x9-inch piece of muslin for the angel head
19 inches of 3½-inch-wide ivory lace for the bodice
One skein of Size 3 brown perle cotton for hair
½ yard of 1/16-inch-wide dark green ribbon
⅓-yard strand of pearls
One gold heart charm
Four burgundy ribbon roses
Polyester fiberfill
White crafts glue or hot-glue gun; tracing paper
Brown and rose embroidery floss for eyes and mouth
Tea bags for dyeing fabrics

INSTRUCTIONS
Note: Pattern includes ¼-inch seam allowances. Sew the pieces with right sides together.

Use hot water and tea bags to make a strong tea solution. Soak muslin and lace in tea solution about 30 minutes. Allow fabrics to dry; press muslin.

Trace the pattern for the angel bust, *above, right.*

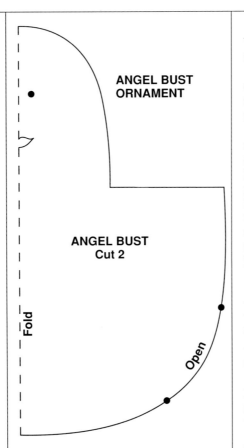

ANGEL BUST ORNAMENT

ANGEL BUST
Cut 2

Fold

Open

CUTTING: Fold muslin in half to measure 3x9 inches; place pattern on fold and cut one bust piece. Reposition pattern and cut second bust piece.

SEWING: Embroider the mouth with rose floss using satin stitches and make French knot eyes using brown floss. Stitch two bust pieces together leaving one side open as indicated. Turn right side out; stuff and stitch the opening closed.

Gather one long edge of lace; place over head and tack around neck with seam in back.

FINISHING: Untwist skein of perle cotton and cut in half. Cut one 6-inch strand of perle cotton for the hanger; knot this strand into a loop and tack to the top of the head.

Twist one-half of skein tightly clockwise until it kinks; fold in half so cut ends are together. Let go of ends; they will twist into each other like the original skein. Tie a thread around the raw ends then glue tied ends to back of head; wrap and tack the skein around the head.

Cut a 9-inch strand of pearls. Weave and glue or tack the strand into the hair.

Make a tiny bow with 2 inches of dark green ribbon; sew or glue to head and attach a ribbon rose to the center of the bow.

Make several 1-inch loops with remaining ribbon; secure center of loops with thread to make bow. Make a loop with the remaining pearl length and add it to the ribbon loops. Stitch the bow to the top center of the lace bodice. Sew three ribbon roses to the center of the looped bow. Sew heart charm below ribbon roses.

Floral Heart Wreath Ornament

Shown on page 21.

Heart wreath measures approximately 5½ inches across at the widest point.

MATERIALS
For one ornament
Spanish moss; dried fern
Florist's wire
18 inches of 1/16-inch-wide burgundy satin ribbon
12 inches of ⅜-inch-wide burgundy satin ribbon
Assorted silk or dried flowers
White crafts glue or hot-glue gun
Sewing thread to match Spanish moss; needle
10 inches of gold metallic thread for hanger

INSTRUCTIONS
Bend florist's wire into a 5x5-inch heart shape. Cover wire with Spanish moss then wrap it with sewing thread. Lay dried fern over the top of the heart; secure with thread.

Beginning at the center top of the heart, wrap the 1/16-inch ribbon around the heart; tie the ends together at the top.

Glue ends of flowers into the wreath. Make a bow from ⅜-inch ribbon and glue to the center top of the heart.

Sew the gold metallic thread through the top of the wreath; tie into a loop for hanging.

Floral Bow Ornament

Shown on page 21.

Bow ornament measures approximately 8 inches long.

MATERIALS
For one ornament
1 yard of 1-inch-wide burgundy or mauve satin ribbon
Dried fern
Silk or dried flowers
Fabric stiffening and draping liquid
Waxed paper; florist's wire
White crafts glue
10 inches of gold metallic thread

INSTRUCTIONS
Apply stiffening solution with fingers to both sides of ribbon. Make a double loop bow, leaving the tails approximately 6 inches long; wipe off excess solution. Place on waxed paper, arranging bow shape as ribbon dries.

Wrap florist's wire around fern stems, leaving wire tails. Wire fern to front of bow by wrapping ends of wire over center of bow several times. Cut silk or dried flowers and leaves from their main stems, leaving short stems. Wire and glue flowers and leaves together; shape as desired. Wrap the end of florist's wire over the center of bow as with the fern.

Thread the gold metallic thread through the wire at the center of the bow; tie into a loop.

Lucky Bird Nest Ornament

Shown on page 21.

The bird nest is approximately 3½ inches in diameter.

MATERIALS
For one ornament
Spanish moss for nest
Sewing thread to match moss
Needle; florist's wire
Small dried flowers
3-inch-long artificial bird
One cinnamon stick
White crafts glue

INSTRUCTIONS
Make a 3½-inch-diameter nest from Spanish moss. Secure the nest shape using a threaded needle to weave thread around and through the moss.

Fasten the cinnamon stick to the bottom of the nest with florist's wire. Leave 3 inches of each side of the wire hanging out beneath the cinnamon stick for attaching the nest to the tree branch.

Glue the base of the bird to the nest. Push a few small dried flowers into the nest beside the bird.

Miniature Topiary Ornament

Shown on page 21.

Topiary measures approximately 5½ inches tall.

MATERIALS
For one ornament
1⅞-inch-tall clay pot (available in gardening stores)
One 1-inch-diameter plastic foam ball
One 1½-inch-diameter plastic foam ball
4½-inch length of 3/16-inch-diameter wood dowel
Spanish moss; potpourri
Raw sienna acrylic paint; cloth scrap to apply paint
White crafts glue
Hot-glue gun
Miniature wood clothespin
24 inches of ¼-inch-wide burgundy or dark green satin ribbon
Small straight pins

INSTRUCTIONS
Use the cloth to apply a thin coat of paint to the dowel and clothespin; let dry.

Cover the 1-inch foam ball with glue; insert into pot. Glue and insert one end of the dowel into the ball in the pot. Pin one end of ribbon to foam ball in pot and glue to bottom of the dowel. Wrap the ribbon around the dowel in a spiral; hot-glue the ribbon to the top of the dowel; trim excess ribbon.

Arrange Spanish moss around the top of the pot to cover the foam ball.

Poke a ½-inch-deep hole in the 1½-inch foam ball with the dowel; remove ball from dowel. Cover ball with glue, then roll in potpourri. Press more potpourri onto ball as needed to cover; let dry. Add glue to hole in potpourri ball and press onto top of dowel.

Make a bow of several loops with remaining ribbon; pin and glue to top of potpourri ball.

Hot-glue miniature clothespin to the bottom of the pot for the fastener.

Smocked Ball Ornament

Shown on page 22.

Ball ornament measures 3 inches in diameter.

MATERIALS
For one ornament
3-inch-diameter plastic foam ball
6½x32-inch piece of ivory batiste
2 yards of ⅜-inch-wide flat ivory lace
⅔ yard of ¼-inch-wide ivory satin ribbon
⅓ yard *each* of ¼-inch-wide seafoam green and mauve satin ribbon
Eighty-four 2.5-mm-diameter pearls
Two 3-inch-long pearl-head pins
One skein *each* of DMC embroidery floss in the following colors: No. 503 seafoam green, No. 316 mauve, and ecru
Size 8 crewel needle
Ivory sewing thread
Ivory quilting thread (for pleating fabric)

INSTRUCTIONS
Note: Use a fabric pleating machine to pleat the fabric before starting. If a pleating machine isn't available, you can use a local or mail-order pleating service.

PREPARING THE FABRIC: Using a tiny zigzag stitch, sew ivory lace to both long edges of the batiste rectangle.

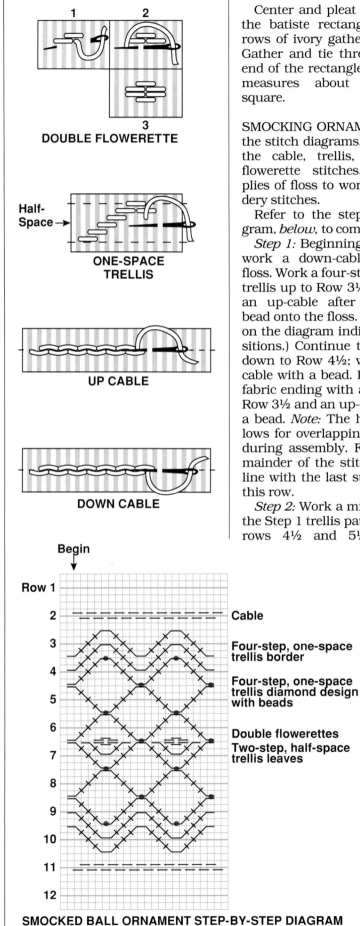

DOUBLE FLOWERETTE

ONE-SPACE TRELLIS

Half-Space→

UP CABLE

DOWN CABLE

Begin

Row 1

2 — Cable

3 — Four-step, one-space trellis border

4 — Four-step, one-space trellis diamond design with beads

5

6 — Double flowerettes

7 — Two-step, half-space trellis leaves

8

9

10

11

12

SMOCKED BALL ORNAMENT STEP-BY-STEP DIAGRAM

Center and pleat the length of the batiste rectangle using 12 rows of ivory gathering threads. Gather and tie threads on each end of the rectangle so the piece measures about 6½ inches square.

SMOCKING ORNAMENT: Follow the stitch diagrams, *left,* to work the cable, trellis, and double flowerette stitches. Use three plies of floss to work all embroidery stitches.

Refer to the step-by-step diagram, *below,* to complete the ball.

Step 1: Beginning on Row 4½, work a down-cable with ecru floss. Work a four-step, one-space trellis up to Row 3½. Next, work an up-cable after threading a bead onto the floss. (The red dots on the diagram indicate bead positions.) Continue trellis pattern down to Row 4½; work a down-cable with a bead. Repeat across fabric ending with a trellis up to Row 3½ and an up-cable without a bead. *Note:* The half-repeat allows for overlapping the pattern during assembly. Finish the remainder of the stitched rows in line with the last stitch made in this row.

Step 2: Work a mirror image of the Step 1 trellis pattern between rows 4½ and 5½, threading beads on the down-cables only. Do not thread a bead on the last down-cable.

Step 3: Repeat Step 1 between rows 5½ and 6½, threading beads on the down-cables only. Do not thread bead on first down-cable.

Step 4: Repeat Step 2 between rows 6½ and 7½.

Step 5: Repeat Step 3 between rows 7½ and 8½.

Step 6: Repeat Step 2 between rows 8½ and 9½.

Step 7: Beginning with a down-cable on Row 4, work a four-step, one-space trellis between rows 3 and 4 with mauve floss.

Step 8: Mirror Step 7 between rows 9 and 10.

Step 9: Repeat Step 7 using seafoam green floss between rows 2½ and 3½.

Step 10: Mirror Step 9 between rows 9½ and 10½.

Step 11: Cable rows 2 and 11.

Step 12: Work mauve double flowerettes in center of diamonds along Row 6½.

Step 13: Work a two-step, half-space trellis leaf design under each flower between rows 6½ and 7 using seafoam green floss.

After smocking is completed, remove gathering threads from rows 3 through 10 only.

ASSEMBLING BALL: Pull the gathering threads from unstitched pleats on each end so threads run through stitched pleats on rows 1, 2, 11, and 12 only. Wrap the smocked panel around foam ball turning under and overlapping ends so smocked pattern lines up evenly. Pin the edges to hold. Pull up gathering threads on rows 1, 2, 11, and 12 as tightly as possible; tie securely and clip thread ends. Blindstitch seam closed.

For streamers, cut one 12-inch length each of seafoam green, mauve, and ivory ribbons. Push a pearl-head pin into each ribbon at the approximate halfway point; part the ruffles at the end at the bottom of the ornament and stick the pin all the way into the ball.

For the hanging loop, cut a 12-inch length of ivory ribbon, overlap the ends and pin into the top of the ball as for the streamers.

Crocheted Hat Ornament

Shown on page 20.

Hat is 5 inches in diameter.

MATERIALS
J. & P. Coats Knit-Cro-Sheen mercerized crochet cotton (400-yard ball): 1 ball of ecru (No. 61)
Size 7 steel crochet hook or size to obtain gauge below
Three mauve ribbon roses
18 inches of ¼-inch-wide mauve satin ribbon
Fabric stiffening and draping solution; paper cup to block
Hot-glue gun
Gold thread

Abbreviations: See page 73.
Gauge: Over rows of dc: 8 dc = 1 inch; 4 rows = 1 inch.

INSTRUCTIONS
Ch 6, join with sl st to form ring.
Rnd 1: Ch 3, work 15 dc in ring; join with sl st to top of beg ch-3.
Rnd 2: Ch 1, sc in same place as joining; (ch 3, sk dc, sc in next dc) 7 times, ch 3; join with sl st in first sc.
Rnd 3: Sl st into ch-3 sp, ch 3; in same sp work 2 dc, ch 2, and 3 dc; (make 3 dc, ch 2, 3 dc in next ch-3 sp) 7 times; join with sl st to top of beg ch-3.
Rnd 4: Sl st into next 2 dc and ch-2 sp; sc in same sp; (ch 7, sc in next ch-2 sp) 7 times, ch 7; join with sl st in first sc.
Rnd 5: Sl st in first ch-7 sp, ch 3, work 6 dc in same sp; work 7 dc in each ch-7 sp around; join to top of beg ch-3.
Rnd 6: Ch 3, dc in each dc around; join to top of beg ch-3.
Rnd 7: Ch 3, dc in same place as join; (dc in next 6 dc, 2 dc in next dc) 7 times, dc in last 6 dc; join to top of beg ch-3.
Rnd 8: Ch 1, sc in same place as join; (ch 9, sk 7 dc, sc in next dc) 7 times, ch 9; join with sl st in first sc.
Rnd 9: In each ch-9 sp, **work sc, 2 hdc, 9 dc, 2 hdc, and sc—scallop made;** join to first sc.
Rnd 10: Ch 11, * sk 6 sts, sc in next st, ch 7, trc in first sc of next scallop, ch 7; rep from * around; end with ch 3, trc in fourth ch of beg ch-11.
Rnd 11: Sc in join; (ch 9, sc in next lp) around; end with ch 4, dtr (yo hook three times) in first sc.
Rnd 12: Sc in join; (ch 11, sc in next lp) around; end with ch 11, sl st in first sc.
Rnd 13: Ch 1, sc in join; * ch 4, in next ch-11 lp work 3 dc, **ch 4, sl st in third ch from hook—picot made,** ch 1, and 3 dc; ch 4, sc in next sc; rep from * around; end with sl st in first sc; fasten off.

BLOCKING THE HAT: Soak hat in stiffening solution. Cut 1 inch off base of paper cup; invert and place crown of hat over cup bottom. Lay brim out flat until dry.

DECORATING HAT: Weave the mauve ribbon through sps in Rnd 7; tie in a bow. Hot-glue three ribbon roses in center of bow.
Thread gold thread through a picot in edging; tie into loop.

Crocheted Fan Ornament

Shown on page 20.

Fan is 5½ inches across at the widest point.

MATERIALS
J. & P. Coats Knit-Cro-Sheen mercerized crochet cotton (400-yard ball): 1 ball of ecru (No. 61)
Size 7 steel crochet hook or size to obtain gauge below
Four mauve ribbon roses
2 yards of assorted ⅛-inch-wide satin ribbons (mauve, green, and wine); embroidery floss to match ribbon; gold thread
Fabric stiffening and draping solution; hot-glue gun

Abbreviations: See page 73.
Gauge: Over rows of dc: 8 dc = 1 inch; 4 rows = 1 inch.

INSTRUCTIONS
Ch 8; join with sl st to form ring. Ch 1, make 16 dc in ring, sl st into beg ch-1. Now, work back and forth in rows as follows.

Row 1: Ch 3, dc in same st as joining; (2 dc in next dc) 5 times; ch 3, turn—12 dc.
Row 2: Dc in first dc; (dc in next dc, 2 dc in next dc) 5 times; dc in ch-3 at end; ch 3, turn—18 dc.
Row 3: Sk first dc, dc in next dc, (ch 1, dc in next 2 dc) 8 times; ch 3, turn.
Rows 4–10: Rep Row 3, having 1 more ch between dc groups on each row; ending with a total of 8 ch between each 2 dc on Row 10; ch 1 to turn at end of last row.
Row 11: Sc in first 2 dc; * in ch-8 lp, work 2 hdc, 5 dc, **ch 3, sl st in top of last dc—picot made;** 4 dc, and 2 hdc; sc in next 2 dc; rep from * across; fasten off.

DECORATING FAN: Apply stiffening solution to fan; shape and lay flat to dry.

Starting at the outside ch-8 lp, weave mauve ribbon over and under each ch-lp; then weave ribbon back up the next row of ch-lps; cut ribbon and tie. Repeat three times more for remaining six rows of ch-lps. Hot-glue a ribbon rose over the ribbon knot at the top of the ch-lps.

Cut 16-inch lengths of ribbon, floss, and gold thread. Loop this assortment of colored ribbon and threads through the crocheted ring at the bottom of the fan from front to back; pull thread and ribbon ends through loop and tighten. Add a gold hanging loop to the top of the fan.

Crocheted Basket Ornament

Shown on page 20.

Basket is 4 inches high.

MATERIALS
J. & P. Coats Knit-Cro-Sheen mercerized crochet cotton (400-yard ball): 1 ball of ecru (No. 61)
Size 7 steel crochet hook or size to obtain gauge below
Six mauve ribbon roses
1 yard of ¼-inch-wide mauve satin ribbon
Hot-glue gun
Fabric stiffening and draping solution; paper cups to block

Abbreviations: See page 73.
Gauge: Over rows of dc: 8 dc = 1 inch; 4 rows = 1 inch.

INSTRUCTIONS

BASKET: Ch 6, join with sl st to form ring.

Rnd 1: Ch 3, work 15 dc in ring; join with sl st to top of beg ch-3.

Rnd 2: Ch 1, sc in same place as joining; (ch 3, sk dc, sc in nest dc) 7 times, ch 3; join with sl st in first sc.

Rnd 3: Sl st in ch-3 sp; ch 3, in same sp work 2 dc, ch 2, and 3 dc; (make 3 dc, ch 2, and 3 dc in next ch-3 sp) 7 times; join with sl st to top of beg ch-3.

Rnd 4: Sl st in next 2 dc and in ch-2 sp, ch 12; (dc in next ch-2 sp, ch 9) 7 times; join with sl st in third ch of beg ch-12.

Rnd 5: In each ch-9 sp around work sc, **2 hdc, 9 dc, 2 hdc, and sc—scallop made;** join to first sc.

Rnd 6: Ch 11, * sk 6 sts, sc in next st, ch 7, trc in first sc of next scallop, ch 7; rep from * around, end with ch 3, trc in fourth ch of beg ch-11.

Rnd 7: Sc in join; (ch 9, sc in next lp) around; end with ch 4, dtr (yo hook three times) in first sc.

Rnd 8: Sc in join; (ch 11, sc in next lp) around; end with ch 11, sl st in first sc.

Rnd 9: Ch 1, sc in join, * ch 4, in next ch-11 lp, work 3 dc; **ch 4, sl st in third ch from hook—picot made;** ch 1, and 3 dc; ch 4, sc in next sc; rep from * around; end with sl st in first sc; fasten off.

HANDLE: *Row 1:* Ch 5, trc in fifth ch from hook, (ch 4, turn, trc in last trc made) 14 times; ch 1, turn—15 sps.

Row 2: Sc in last trc just made, 2 sc in first sp, * in next sp, work 3 dc, picot, ch 1, and 3 dc; sc in next sp; rep from * 6 times more, work 4 sc in end sp; rep from * across other side of handle, ending with 2 sc in last sp; sl st in first sc made; fasten off.

BLOCKING BASKET: Soak both pieces in stiffening solution. Invert paper cup and place doily basket over paper cup bottom to shape basket. Evenly adjust the fullness of the doily along the sides of the cup. Set aside to dry.

Lay the handle flat to dry for an hour. Before the handle is completely dry, lay it gently over the side of another paper cup. Let it finish drying.

DECORATING THE BASKET: Cut two 12-inch pieces of ribbon to weave along the rim of the basket. Start each ribbon in the same space and weave them in opposite directions, in and out of the spaces between shells of Rnd 9. End each ribbon in the space directly opposite the starting point on the rim. Tie the tails into bows on opposite sides of the basket.

Cut a piece of ribbon that is 4 inches longer than the handle; weave ribbon in and out of spaces along center of handle. Wrap the 2-inch tails a few times through the two spaces behind the bows on the basket rim; trim excess and hot-glue the ends inside handle next to basket rim.

Hot-glue three ribbon roses above each bow.

If desired, place potpourri in net bags or candy inside the basket and hang using the handle.

Beaded Split-Ring Tatted Ball Cover

Shown on page 22.

Cover fits a 2- to 2½-inch-diameter glass ball ornament.

MATERIALS
For one ball cover
DMC Size 5 ecru perle cotton thread; DMC Size 8 ecru perle cotton thread; two tatting shuttles
510 peach iridescent seed beads; beading needle

Abbreviations: See page 35.

INSTRUCTIONS
Note: Read split-ring tatting instructions on page 34.

Mark shuttles A and B. Wind shuttle A with 7 yards of Size 5 perle cotton. Cut and start winding 6 yards of Size 8 perle cotton onto shuttle B. String beads onto shuttle B thread with beading needle; finish winding thread.

CENTER RING: Leaving a 6-inch tail, make a r of: 1, (p, 2) 47 times; p, 1, clr. Cut thread, leaving a 6-inch tail; tie a square knot and sew threads back into wrong side of ring. Trim excess thread and dab with crafts glue. *Note:* The picots in this ring are all ½ inch long after being closed.

SPLIT-RING AND BEADED ROUND: Begin by leaving a 6-inch tail with both shuttles; knot tails together.

Step 1: Using shuttle A, work sr of 6, join to first p of Center Ring, 6, rs. Using shuttle B, work 16, clsr; dnrw.

Step 2: Using shuttle A, work sr of 6, join to fourth p of Center Ring, 6, rs. Using shuttle B, work 4, push 25 beads up from shuttle (this makes a long beaded p), 4, push 35 beads up from shuttle, 4, push 25 beads up from shuttle, 4, clsr; dnrw.

Step 3: Rep Step 1, joining to eighth p of Center Ring.

Step 4: Rep Step 2, joining to twelfth p of Center Ring.

Continue to rep steps 1 and 2 until six plain sr and six beaded r have been completed, making sure that you skip 3 more p each step; end leaving a 6-inch tail. Tie tails in square knots and sew ends into wrong side of tatting.

Fabric-Covered Ball Ornament

Shown on page 23.

Ball is 3 inches in diameter.

MATERIALS
For one ornament
One 3-inch-diameter plastic foam ball
Scraps of fancy fabrics, including satins, velvets, and brocades
1 yard of gold metallic braid or ribbon (to go around ball)
½ yard of gold metallic ribbon (for bow on top)
White crafts glue; straight pins
Tracing paper

continued on page 35

Split-Ring Tatting

TATTING THE REVERSE PART OF A SPLIT RING: The reverse part of a split ring is an upside-down, backward version of a regularly tatted double stitch. Combined with double stitches, it creates a different-looking tatted ring.

Two shuttles (usually wound with different thread colors) are used for this technique. When practicing, it is easier to learn the hand manipulation if only one shuttle is used and the second shuttle is replaced with a ball of thread of a different color.

Step 1: Position your hands, shuttle, and thread as if preparing to tat a regular chain. Tie the beginning tails together. See Diagram A, *below.*

Step 2: Tat *wrong* stitches. To do this, the fingers of the left hand must *not* be relaxed at any time while throwing the shuttle or pulling on the shuttle thread to form the stitch. The wrong (or upside-down) stitches should be the color of the thread on the shuttle, not the color on the ball of thread.

Note: If you pull the shuttle toward your body to complete the first half of the reverse stitch (as you were taught *not* to do when first learning to tat), you will prevent the thread from "flipping" or "popping" into a regular double stitch.

TATTING A SPLIT RING: *Step 1:* Mark shuttles A and B. Leaving a 4-inch beginning tail, use shuttle A to start a regular tatted ring of 3, p, 3, p, 3; do not close ring. Take the circle thread from the left hand and turn it upside down; let shuttle A dangle. See diagrams B and C, *left.*

Step 2: Return circle thread to hand with the beginning tail hanging up and over the left thumb, with the *first* stitch between thumb and forefinger of the left hand, and with shuttle A dangling. Cross bars of regular stitches and picots should be facing down and to the left or right. Circle thread should be enlarged, but comfortable, before you begin the next step. See Diagram C.

Step 3: Also grasp beginning tail of shuttle B to reverse stitch, beginning next to the first stitch of the regularly tatted stitches. Reverse stitch, 9. See Diagram D.

Remove circle thread from hand. Pull on shuttle A thread to close ring. **The only way to close a split ring is by pulling the thread from the shuttle, *not* by pulling on the beginning tail.** See Diagram E.

Diagram F shows several practice rings in a row. Note that the rings have picots on the regularly tatted side; there are no picots on the reverse-stitch side.

Step 4: Use the same pattern as before to tat picots on the regularly tatted side of the split ring and put two picots on the reverse-stitch side, too. See Diagram G.

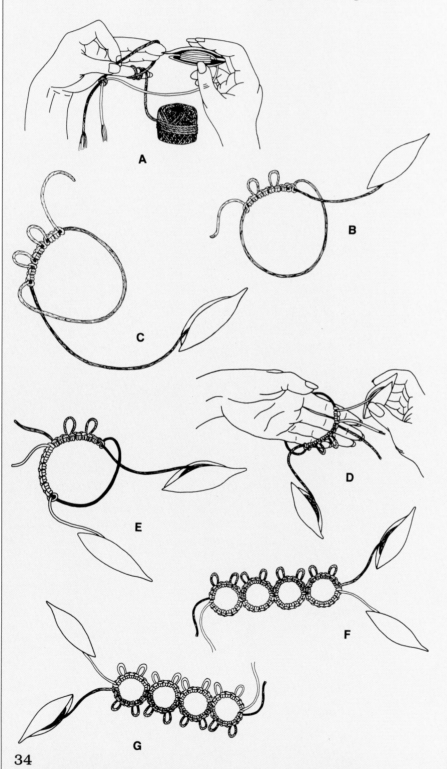

34

Continued from page 33

INSTRUCTIONS

Trace the full-size pattern, *bottom* of page 37, and cut out pattern. Place pattern on the bias of the fabric and draw around pattern; cut out six pieces in assorted fabrics. Add glue to backs of fabric pieces and pin and glue them to ball, stretching fabric slightly so it lies flat against the ball. Overlap edges slightly; trim away excess fabric if necessary. Remove pins after glue has dried.

Cut three 10-inch lengths of braid to cover fabric edges; overlap braid ends and secure with glue and pins at one point on the ball.

Use gold ribbon to make several bow loops; secure center of loops with glue and pin at the point on the ball where the braid overlaps. For hanging, add a longer loop in the center of the bow.

Pierced-Paper Flower Ornament

Shown on pages 24 and 25.

Flower measures 2½ inches in diameter.

MATERIALS
One sheet of 90-pound watercolor paper
Medium-size sewing needle
Crafts knife
Tracing paper
Graphite paper
Towel; cutting surface
Gold metallic thread (hanger)
White crafts glue

INSTRUCTIONS
Trace inner and outer flower patterns on page 37, completing the mirror image of the outer flower by flopping the tracing after the first half is completed. Place graphite paper facedown atop watercolor paper; place tracings over graphite paper. Draw over the pattern lines with a sharp pencil.

Place paper on a cutting surface and use the crafts knife to remove the center cuts that are marked in gray; then cut out the flower designs.

continued

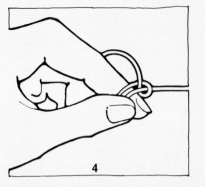
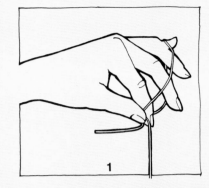
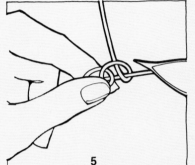
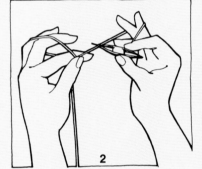
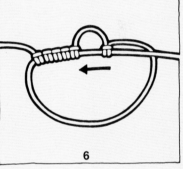
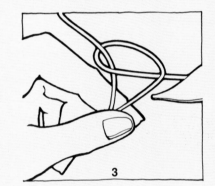

TATTING GUIDE

Tatting Abbreviations

ch .... chain
clr .... close ring
clsr .... close split ring
dnrw .... do not reverse work
p .... picot
r .... ring
rep .... repeat
rs .... reverse stitch

(Set first shuttle aside; remove circle thread from hand, turn it from top to bottom, then return it to left hand; add shuttle B.)

rw .... reverse work
(Turn work just completed upside down.)
sr .... split ring
(If a direction step starts with sr, two shuttles will be used to make next ring. If a step does not start with sr, you will be directed to do only a regularly tatted ring with one shuttle.)
st .... stitch

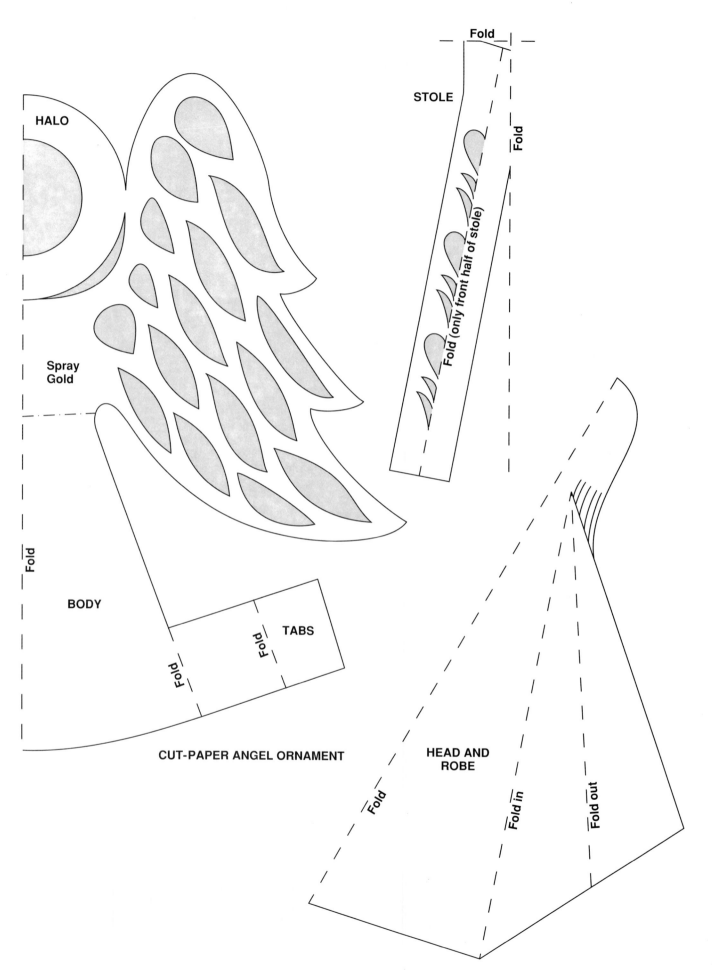

HALO

STOLE

Spray
Gold

Fold (only front half of stole)

Fold

Fold

Fold

BODY

TABS

Fold

Fold

CUT-PAPER ANGEL ORNAMENT

HEAD AND
ROBE

Fold

Fold in

Fold out

Lay right side of design on towel; use needle to punch holes from wrong side of design. With right sides of designs facing, make folds as marked on the pattern.

Glue petal tips and center of inner flower to the outer flower.

Cut a 10-inch piece of gold metallic thread; put thread through tip of one outer petal; tie into loop.

Cut-Paper Angel Ornament

Shown on pages 24 and 25.

Angel measures 7 inches high.

MATERIALS
One 19x25-inch piece of white parchment paper for two ornaments
Gold spray paint for the halo and wings; newspaper
Crafts knife
Glue stick; scissors
10-inch piece of gold metallic thread for the hanger
Tracing paper; graphite paper
Tea bags for dyeing paper

INSTRUCTIONS
Trace body, head and robe, and stole patterns, *opposite*, onto tracing paper. Set aside stole pattern. Fold the parchment paper in half lengthwise. Lay graphite paper atop parchment; place tracings on center folds as indicated and transfer the body and head and robe design lines.

Cut out gray areas as marked on the patterns. Make inside cuts using a sharp crafts knife and outside cuts using scissors.

For the stole, fold a 3x10-inch piece of paper in half lengthwise then widthwise. Then cut out the design only on one side of the stole piece.

Spray paint the upper half of body piece with gold (cover bottom half with newspaper); let dry.

Make a strong tea solution with hot water and tea bags. Dab tea solution on robe and stole. Place pieces between paper towels and place under a book to dry flat.

Fold angel's robe in and out as indicated on pattern. Place stole over head; tuck back half of stole under halo and over wings. Dab glue under front of robe and press to bottom of halo and wing piece.

Bend and glue tabs in back of body piece.

String gold metallic thread through halo to hang from tree.

Tatted Star Ornaments

Shown on pages 24 and 25.

Five-pointed star is 5½ inches in diameter; four-pointed star is 4¾ inches in diameter; six-pointed star is 4¼ inches in diameter.

MATERIALS
DMC Size 8 ecru perle cotton; tatting shuttle
Size 10 steel crochet hook (if no point or hook is on the shuttle)
White crafts glue
Rustproof pins

Abbreviations: See page 35.

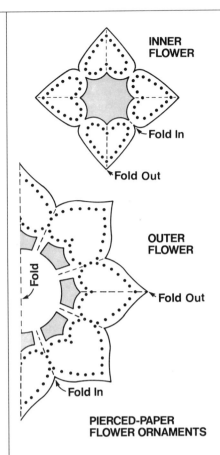

INNER FLOWER
Fold In
Fold Out

OUTER FLOWER
Fold
Fold Out
Fold In

PIERCED-PAPER FLOWER ORNAMENTS

INSTRUCTIONS
Refer to Tatting Guide diagrams on page 35, working from the top to the bottom of each column.

Note: The picots, when opened, should have a diameter of ¼ inch. Leave 6-inch tails at beginning and end of each round. To finish a round, tie tails in 2 square knots. Weave tails back through 2 or 3 stitches. Trim tails. Dab knots with glue.

Tie the ball and shuttle threads together.

continued

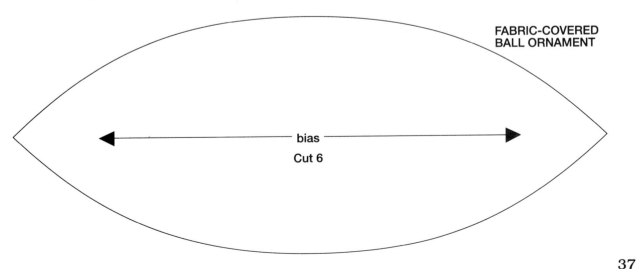

FABRIC-COVERED BALL ORNAMENT

bias

Cut 6

Five-pointed star

Wind 19 yards of perle cotton on shuttle; 4½ yards will be used from the ball.

ROUND 1: *Step 1:* R of 5, (p, 5) 6 times; clr, rw.

Step 2: Ch of 5, (p, 3) 4 times; p, 5, push stitches together to tighten, rw.

Step 3: R of 5 (p, 5) twice; join to fourth p of previous r, 5, (p, 5) 3 times; clr, rw.

Step 4: Rep steps 2 and 3 until there are 5 r and ch.

Step 5: R of 5, (p, 5) twice; join to fourth p of previous r, 5, join to third p of first r, 5, (p, 5) twice; clr, rw.

Step 6: Rep Step 2.

Finish rnd (see editor's note on page 37).

ROUND 2: *Step 1:* R of 5, (p, 5) 4 times; clr, dnrw.

Step 2: Join to center p of any ch of Rnd 1, ch of 10, tighten stitches, dnrw.

Step 3: R of 5, p, 5, join to fourth p of previous r, 5, (p, 5) 3 times; clr, dnrw.

Step 4: Ch of 10, tighten stitches, dnrw.

Step 5: Rep Step 3.

Step 6: Rep Step 4.

Step 7 (first r of cloverleaf at tip): R of 5, p, 5, join to fourth p of previous r, 5, (p, 5) 3 times; clr.

Step 8 (second r of cloverleaf): Start r close to previous r. R of 5, join to last p of previous r, 5, (p, 5) 8 times; clr.

Step 9 (third r of cloverleaf): Start r close to previous r. R of 5, join to last p of previous r, 5, (p, 5) 4 times; clr, dnrw.

Step 10: Ch of 10, tighten stitches, dnrw.

Step 11: R of 5, p, 5, join to fourth p of previous r, 5, (p, 5) 3 times; clr, dnrw.

Step 12: Ch of 10, join to center p of next ch of Rnd 1, tighten stitches, dnrw.

Step 13: R of 5, p, 5, join to fourth p of previous r, 5, (p, 5) 3 times; clr, dnrw.

Step 14: Ch 10, tighten stitches, dnrw.

Step 15: Rep steps 3–14 four times.

Step 16: Rep steps 3–8.

Step 17: R of 5, p, 5, join to fourth p of previous r, 5, p, 5, join to second p of first r of Rnd 2, 5, p, 5, clr, dnrw.

Step 18: Ch of 10, join to middle p of last ch of Rnd 1, tighten stitches. Finish rnd.

FINISHING: Stretch and pin tatting to a cloth-covered board using rustproof pins. Stiffen back side with a mixture that is 2 parts white crafts glue to 1 part water.

Four-pointed star

Wind 8 yards of perle cotton on shuttle; 4½ yards will be used from the ball.

ROUND 1: *Step 1:* R of 5, (p, 5) 5 times; clr.

Step 2: R of 5, join to last p of previous r, 5, (p, 5) 4 times; clr.

Step 3: Rep Step 2.

Step 4: R of 5, join to last p of previous r, 5, (p, 5) 3 times; join to first p of first r, 5, clr, rw.

Finish rnd.

ROUND 2: *Step 1:* Prepare to tat a ch. Join to fourth p of any r of Rnd 1 and continue with ch of 4, p, 4, join to next p of next r to right, tighten stitches.

Step 2: Ch of 5, (p, 5) 3 times; join to fourth p of same r, tighten stitches.

Step 3: Ch of 4, p, 4, join to second p of next r to right, tighten stitches.

Step 4: Rep steps 2 and 3 until all of Rnd 1 is encased in a continuous ch and end is joined in same p as beginning. Finish rnd.

ROUND 3: *Step 1:* R of 10, with 1 of the points of the completed square facing you, join to right p of 1 of the corners, 10, clr, rw.

Step 2: Ch of 4, (p, 4) 4 times; tighten stitches.

Step 3: R of 10, skip 1 p, join to left p of next corner of completed square, 10, clr, rw.

Step 4: Ch of 4, (p, 4) 5 times; tighten stitches, dnrw.

Step 5: R of 5, join to last p of previous ch, 5, (p, 5) twice; clr, dnrw. Start next r as close to previous r as possible.

Step 6: R of 5, join to last p of previous r, 10, p, 10, p, 5, clr, dnrw. Start next r close to previous r.

Step 7: R of 5, join to last p of previous r, 5, (p, 5) twice; clr, dnrw.

Step 8: Ch of 4, join to last p of previous r, 4, (p, 4) times; tighten stitches, rw.

Step 9: R of 10, join to second p to right of previous join to Rnd 2, 10, clr, rw.

Step 10: Ch of 4, (p, 4) 4 times; tighten stitches, rw.

Step 11: Rep steps 3–10 twice.

Step 12: Rep steps 3–8.

Finish rnd. See finishing instructions for five-pointed star, *left.*

Six-pointed star

Wind 19 yards of perle cotton on shuttle; 4½ yards will be used from the ball. This ornament is tatted in a single round.

Step 1: R of 5, (p, 5) 3 times; clr, rw.

Step 2: Ch of 5, p, 5, rw.

Step 3: R of 5, join to last p of previous r, 5, (p, 5) twice; clr, rw.

Step 4: Ch of 4, p, 4, rw.

Step 5: R of 5, join to last p of previous r, 5, (p, 5) twice; clr, rw.

Step 6: Ch of 3, rw.

Step 7: R of 5, join to last p of previous r, 5, (p, 5) 4 times, clr, rw.

Step 8: Ch of 3, rw.

Step 9: R of 5, join to last p of previous r, 5, (p, 5) twice; clr, rw.

Step 10: ch of 4, join to p of third previous ch, 4, rw.

Step 11: R of 5, join to last p of previous r, 5, (p, 5) twice; clr, rw.

Step 12: Ch of 5, join to p of fifth previous ch, 5, rw.

Step 13: R of 5, join to last p of previous r, 5, (p, 5) twice; clr, rw.

Step 14: Ch of 10, dnrw.

Step 15: R of 5, (p, 5) 5 times; clr, dnrw.

Step 16: Ch of 10, rw.

Step 17: R of 5, p, 5, join to center p of second previous r, 5, p, 5, clr, rw.

Step 18: Rep steps 2–14.

Step 19: R of 5, p, 5, join to next to last p of eighth previous r, 5, (p, 5) 3 times; clr, dnrw.

Step 20: Rep steps 16 and 17.

Step 21: Rep (steps 2–14, 19, 16, and 17 in this order) 3 times.

Step 22: Rep steps 2–12.

Step 23: R of 5, join to last p of previous r, 5, join to middle p of first r, 5, p, 5, clr, rw.

Step 24: Ch of 10, dnrw.

Step 25: R of 5, p, 5, join to

fourth p of eighth previous r, 5, p, 5, join to second p of (adjacent) eighth r from beg, 5, p, 5, clr, dnrw.

Step 26: Ch of 10.

Finish rnd. See finishing instructions for five-pointed star, *opposite.*

Victorian Santa Ornament

Shown on page 25.

Santa measures 7 inches high.

MATERIALS
For one ornament
10x12-inch piece of burgundy velvet for body and arms
9x4-inch piece of quilt batting
17x½-inch imitation fur for robe and hood trim
2x4-inch piece of black velvet for boots
Tracing paper
Small amount of cleaned raw wool or roving for beard
2-inch square of muslin for face
Small jingle bell
One piece of imitation greenery; miniature pinecone; miniature pipe cleaner candy cane
Brown-ink fabric pen; rose fabric paint; liner brush
10-inch strand gold thread for the hanger

INSTRUCTIONS
PREPARATION AND CUTTING: *Note:* Patterns include ¼-inch seam allowances.

Fold tracing paper in half and place on fold line of pattern; trace full-size body and face/boot patterns, *right.* Cut out patterns.

Fold burgundy velvet in half widthwise; lay body pattern atop velvet and cut around pattern. Cut a 10½x2-inch velvet strip for arms.

Cut one face/boot and one body from batting; save excess batting for stuffing boots.

Cut two boots from the black velvet.

Cut one face from muslin. Draw eyes and nose on fabric with brown pen. Paint on rose lips and cheeks.

ASSEMBLY: Trim the batting circle a little smaller than the face; position and layer the face and batting atop the right side of one of the body pieces. Sew the face to the body, stitching along the edge of the face. The edge will be covered with fur so it's not necessary to turn it under.

For the arms, fold both long edges of the velvet strip toward the center, overlapping them slightly. Tie a loose knot in the center of the arm strip for hands. Sew the short edges of the arms to opposite sides of the body front as marked on the pattern.

Make the boots by sewing a running stitch around the edges of each black velvet circle; place some batting in the center of the wrong side of the velvet and draw thread up to gather boot into a ball shape. With the excess thread, tack the boots to the center bottom front of the body as indicated on the pattern.

With right sides facing, place the body back next to the body front then place the batting against the wrong side of the body back; pin all layers together. Sew around sides and top of Santa. Leave bottom open for turning. Make sure that the loose parts of the arms remain free of the seam. Turn right sides out.

Turn bottom edges up with the feet sticking out. Whipstitch bottom edges closed.

Using small concealing stitches, sew a strip of fur trim around the bottom of Santa's robe. Sew remaining fur up the center of the robe and around the face, covering the raw edges and stitches.

FINISHING: Tack wool to the face below the mouth for a beard; tack a tiny strand of wool beneath the nose for a mustache.

Sew the bell to the tip of the hat, as indicated on pattern; tie the gold thread through the bell and into a loop.

Tack the greens, pinecone, and candy cane to the body behind one of the arms. Tack the arms to the body at the hand knot.

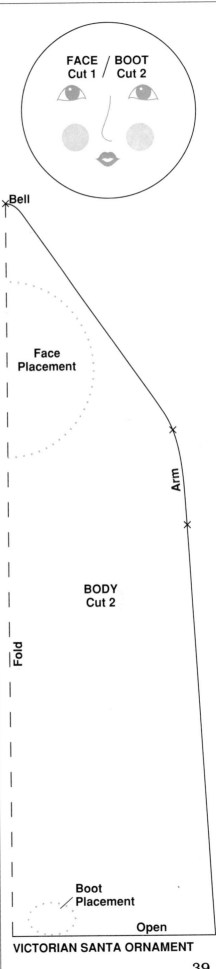

FACE / BOOT
Cut 1 / Cut 2

Bell

Face Placement

Arm

BODY
Cut 2

Fold

Boot
Placement

Open

VICTORIAN SANTA ORNAMENT

HOLIDAY CRITTERS

A WOODLAND CARNIVAL

No matter what your favorite crafting technique—painted wood, cross-stitch, stuffed fabric, or dough art—these next pages are filled with an assortment of winsome animal ornaments from which to choose.

Playing in the boughs of an outdoor pine, the cross-stitched creatures, *right,* are stitched on perforated paper. When your stitching is complete, cut out the shapes and hang them with gold thread on your indoor tree.

Try your hand at the three animals, *below.*

They're cut from tempered hardboard using a jigsaw, then painted with acrylic paints.

Instructions for these ornaments begin on page 44.

Use favorite scraps of fabric to make the lovable menagerie of bears, bunnies, cats, and geese that trims the handle of the basket, *above.* For special touches, add bright satin ribbons and tiny red hearts.

You'll have a delightful time creating the critters, *opposite,* from flour, salt, water, and tea to trim your tree or decorate your packages. Shape and bake the bear parts a few at a time, adding bits of paper clips, netting, toothpicks,

blocks, and pinecones to make these dough ornaments even more special.

Instructions for the dough bears begin on page 44. Directions for the country stuffed animal ornaments begin on page 47.

Cross-Stitched Winter Wonderland Critters

Shown on pages 40 and 41.

All of the ornaments are approximately 5 inches high.

MATERIALS
Four 9x12-inch sheets of white perforated paper
One skein each of DMC embroidery floss in colors listed on the color key
Crafts knife; scissors
Four 8-inch lengths of gold thread; tapestry needle

INSTRUCTIONS
Using the arrows on the charts as a guide, locate the center of each design; begin stitching here. Center and stitch each ornament on a sheet of perforated paper. After all stitching is completed, the outside and unstitched inside areas are cut away with the crafts knife or scissors. Refer to the diagram *below* to work the cross-stitches. See diagram on page 47 to work backstitches.

Charts of the four animals are *opposite* and on page 46. Use three strands of floss to work cross-stitches and two strands of floss to work backstitches.

For the skunk, backstitch the body with No. 310 black. Backstitch skis with No. 824 royal blue. Backstitch poles, hat, and scarf with No. 606 red-orange.

For the beaver, backstitch the body, eyes, teeth, hat, and mittens with No. 844 black-brown. Backstitch the beaver's feet with black. For the snowman, backstitch the body, mouth, and teeth with No.

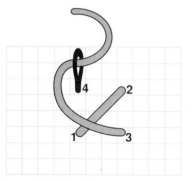

CROSS-STITCH

931 dark ice blue. Backstitch the carrot nose with No. 720 dark orange. Backstitch the hat with black.

For the rat, backstitch the body using No. 844 black-brown. Backstitch the hat and scarf with No. 666 true red. Backstitch the tongue with No. 3705 coral. Backstitch the snowball with No. 931 dark ice blue. Work French knots on the scarf as indicated by the shaded square with 3 strands of true red. See the diagram on page 67 to work the French knots.

For the raccoon, backstitch the body with No. 838 brown. Backstitch the scarf, skirt, and hat with No. 562 blue-green. Backstitch the skates with No. 310 black. Backstitch laces on the left skate with No. 349 red. Work a French knot in the center of the eye with three strands of No. 844 black-brown.

FINISHING: Cut out the unstitched areas inside the designs with the crafts knife.

Use the scissors to cut around each ornament one square beyond the stitching, leaving one square with a hole at the top center of each ornament for the hanging thread. Insert an 8-inch length of gold thread into the hole and tie into a loop.

Playful Bear Dough Ornaments

Shown on page 43.

MATERIALS
2 cups flour; ½ cup salt
2 tablespoons instant tea
Water; two bowls
Red, green, white, and blue acrylic paints
India ink; fine-tipped pen
Assorted paintbrushes
Garlic press
Polyurethane varnish spray
White crafts glue
Paper clips; toothpick
Scraps of nylon net; pinecone
Wood baby block

INSTRUCTIONS
DOUGH: For the brown bears, place 1 cup of flour and ¼ cup of salt into a bowl with 2 tablespoons of instant tea. In the second bowl, make another batch of dough without the tea for the white parts of the ornaments.

Add 6 tablespoons of hot tap water to the dry ingredients in each bowl. *Note:* Amount of water may vary with temperature and humidity. Add enough water to make dough soft and workable, but not sticky. Knead until all salt is worked in and dough feels smooth.

For the ballerina, skater, and skier bears
Referring to the photo on page 43, form the parts of the body by rolling small amounts of dough in your palms and shaping. Moisten the dough where pieces touch.

For the skater bear, cut two paper clips apart to make the ice-skate blades; push paper clip halves into toes of the bear.

For the skier bear, push a toothpick into the bear's hands for the pole, make a small disk of clay and push it onto the bottom of the toothpick.

For hanging all ornaments, insert the U-shaped portion of a paper clip in the top of the bear before baking.

Bake at 275 degrees for about 2½ hours; check periodically. The ornaments are done when they are completely hard. Allow ornaments to cool.

Paint the ornaments using the acrylic paints and referring to the photograph on page 43 for ideas. Draw faces with the fine-tipped pen and ink. Use red paint and water to make a semitransparent wash for blushing the cheeks.

Spray polyurethane varnish over the finished bears.

To finish the ballerina bears, cut a 1¼x14-inch strip of nylon net. Sew a running stitch down the middle of the length of the strip; pull to gather and fit around body. Glue it to bear after varnish has dried.

continued

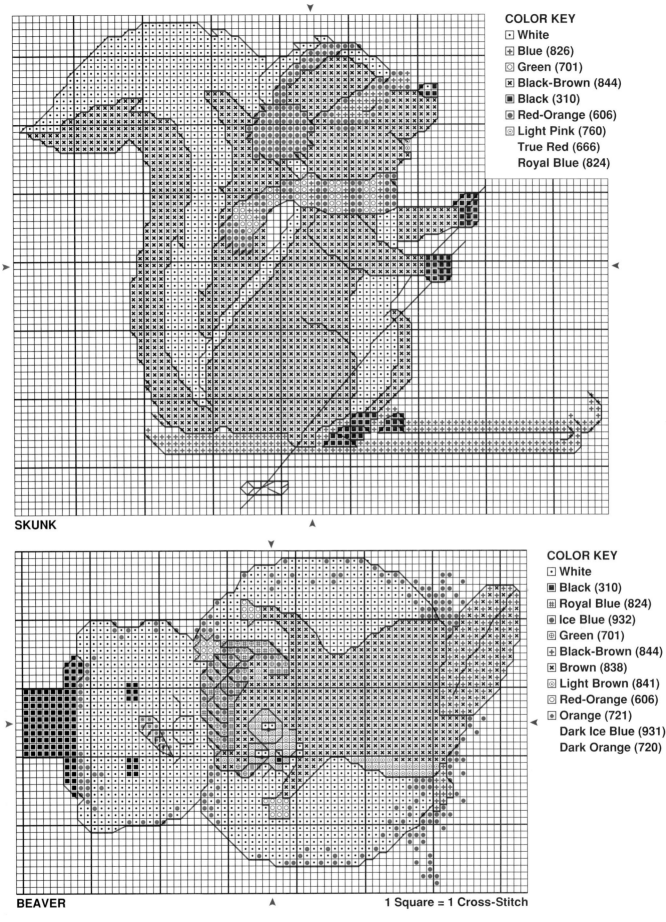

COLOR KEY

· White
⊞ Blue (826)
◎ Green (701)
⊠ Black-Brown (844)
■ Black (310)
⊡ Red-Orange (606)
◉ Light Pink (760)
  True Red (666)
  Royal Blue (824)

SKUNK

COLOR KEY

· White
■ Black (310)
⊞ Royal Blue (824)
⊡ Ice Blue (932)
⊕ Green (701)
⊞ Black-Brown (844)
⊠ Brown (838)
◎ Light Brown (841)
◉ Red-Orange (606)
◉ Orange (721)
  Dark Ice Blue (931)
  Dark Orange (720)

BEAVER

1 Square = 1 Cross-Stitch

CROSS-STITCHED WINTER WONDERLAND CRITTERS

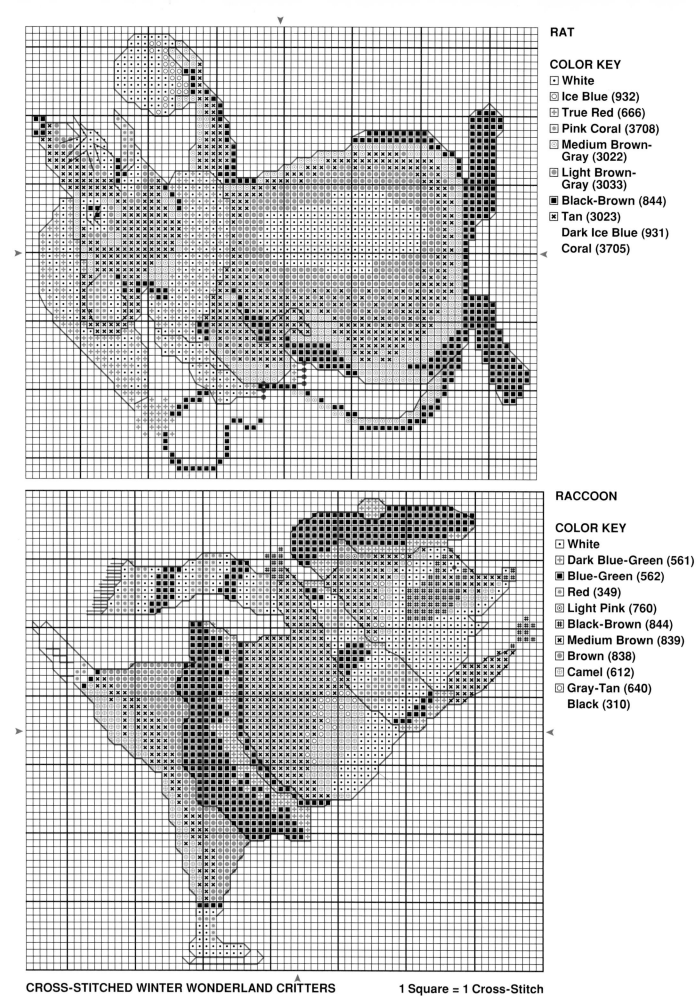

RAT

COLOR KEY
⊡ White
⊚ Ice Blue (932)
⊞ True Red (666)
⊟ Pink Coral (3708)
⊙ Medium Brown-
   Gray (3022)
▨ Light Brown-
   Gray (3033)
■ Black-Brown (844)
⊠ Tan (3023)
   Dark Ice Blue (931)
   Coral (3705)

RACCOON

COLOR KEY
⊡ White
⊞ Dark Blue-Green (561)
■ Blue-Green (562)
▨ Red (349)
⊙ Light Pink (760)
Black-Brown (844)
⊠ Medium Brown (839)
⊚ Brown (838)
⊟ Camel (612)
⊘ Gray-Tan (640)
   Black (310)

CROSS-STITCHED WINTER WONDERLAND CRITTERS   1 Square = 1 Cross-Stitch

For the pinecone and block bears

Referring to the photo on page 43, form the body and attach it to the pinecone or block. Use crumpled aluminum foil to support the pinecone in position in the oven. Bake at 275 degrees for 15 minutes. Remove from the oven and cool.

Add head and legs. Bake for 15 minutes more and cool.

Add arms and bake for another 15 minutes and cool.

Add ears, bows, or other finishing details. Bake for an hour or until done; cool. Paint as desired. Spray with varnish.

Country Stuffed-Animal Ornaments

Shown on page 42.

The bear and bunny measure approximately 3½ inches high; cat and goose measure approximately 4½ inches high.

MATERIALS
To make one of each ornament

Four 8x16-inch pieces of check or print fabrics
Tracing paper
Four 16-inch lengths of ¼-inch-wide satin ribbons
Four 8-inch lengths of gold thread for hangers
Small wooden heart (optional)
Polyester fiberfill
Non-permanent marker

INSTRUCTIONS

Note: The marked lines on the patterns indicate sewing lines. Sew all pieces with right sides facing.

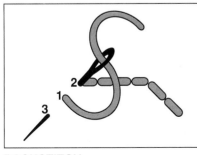

BACKSTITCH

SEWING THE BODIES: Trace the full-size bunny, *below,* and cat and goose patterns on page 48 onto tracing paper; cut out patterns. Fold tracing paper in half and place fold of paper on fold line of bear pattern on page 48. Trace bear and cut out pattern, completing the bear shape.

Fold each of the four fabric pieces in half, right sides facing. Using the non-permanent marker, draw around patterns on fabrics; do not cut out. Stitch atop the drawn lines, leaving openings for turnings as indicated.

Make a narrow zigzag stitch just outside the sewn lines; cut out the animals next to the zigzag stitches. Clip curves; turn ornaments right side out through openings.

Stuff bodies firmly; slip-stitch the openings closed.

THE CAT'S TAIL: Sew and turn the cat's tail in the same manner as the body.

Stuff half of the tail firmly, starting at the tip; then begin decreasing firmness. Turn edges in ¼ inch at the open end of the tail and baste opening closed.

Position and pin the tail to the front of the cat's body. Slip-stitch the turned-under edge of tail to the back of the body; slip-stitch the tail to the front of the body.

FINISHING: Sew an 8-inch gold thread through the top of each animal's head at the seam for the hanger; tie the ends of the thread in a knot.

Tie a bow around the neck of each animal; sew through the knot to keep it from slipping.

If desired, glue a small wooden heart onto each animal's chest.

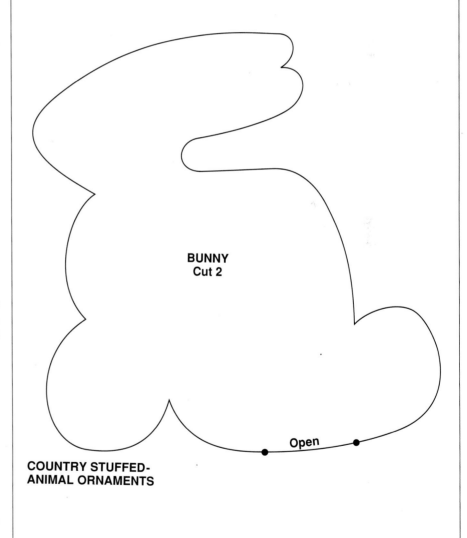

**BUNNY
Cut 2**

Open

**COUNTRY STUFFED-
ANIMAL ORNAMENTS**

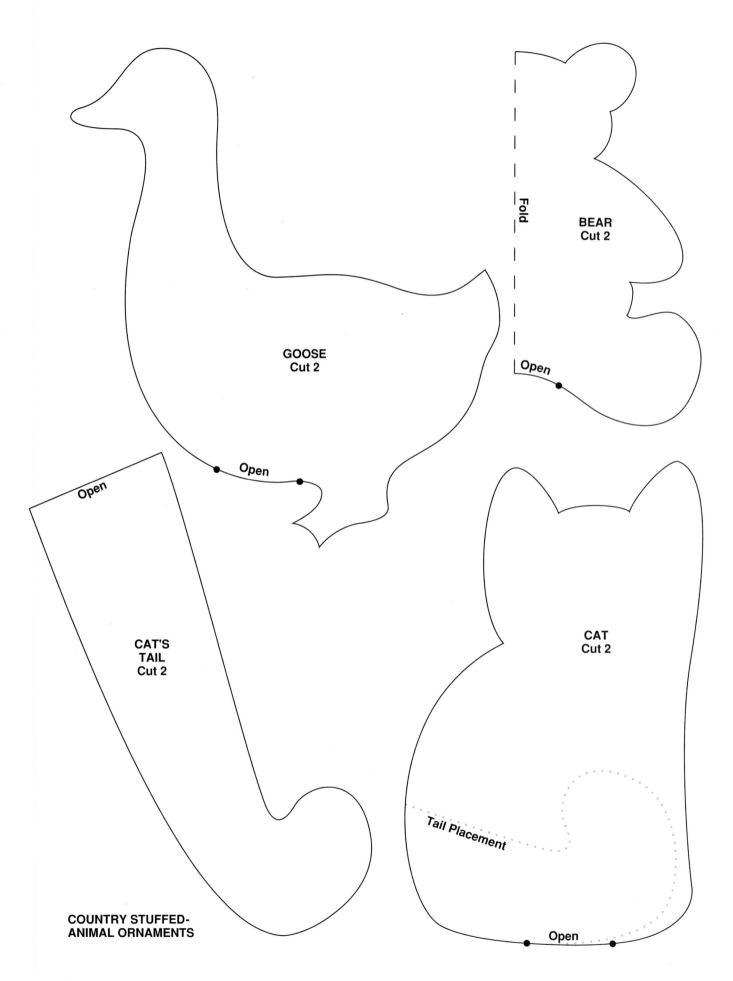

GOOSE
Cut 2

Open

Open

BEAR
Cut 2

Fold

Open

Open

CAT'S
TAIL
Cut 2

CAT
Cut 2

Tail Placement

Open

COUNTRY STUFFED-
ANIMAL ORNAMENTS

Painted Cat And Bear Ornaments

Shown on page 40.

The ornaments measure approximately 3¾ inches high.

MATERIALS
For all three ornaments
6x10-inch piece of ⅛-inch tempered hardboard
Tracing paper; graphite paper
Acrylic paints in the following colors: blue, black, white, yellow ocher, brown, red, and green
Assorted artist's brushes
Paint palette or plate
Paper towels
⅛-inch-diameter drill bit; drill
Jigsaw
Gold cording for hangers

INSTRUCTIONS
Trace the full-size patterns, *below*, onto tracing paper; transfer patterns to hardboard with graphite paper. Cut out ornaments with a jigsaw. Sand smooth. Prime fronts and backs of ornaments with white paint; lightly sand again when dry.

Mix paints with white or black to make light and dark shades of each color.

For the cat
Base-paint the cat white, the bow pink, and the wreath yellow ocher. Paint dark green leaves on the wreath (indicated by black areas on the pattern); paint light green leaves over dark green leaves. Add pink dots for flowers over leaves. On the bow, shade the edges with dark pink; highlight the bow with light pink. Fill in the cat's eyes with blue; add black irises. Use the photo on page 40 as a guide to complete the remaining details.

For the seated bear
Base-paint the bear light brown, the jacket medium blue, and the pants off-white. Paint hearts light red. With medium brown, shade edges on bear's body. Paint inner ears and paws dark brown.

Refer to the photo on page 40 to paint blue and red stripes on the pants, and to shade the pants with blue along the inseam. Shade the outline of the coat with dark blue; shade the edges of the heart with dark red. Add yellow buttons to coat and side of pants. Paint red cheeks, white trims, and black facial details.

For the standing bear
Base-paint the bear's head, neck, ears, hand, and legs light brown; paint the nightgown and slippers medium pink. Use dark pink to shade the nightgown around the arm, under the plate, and at the back of the head. Highlight the arm and ruffles at bottom of nightgown with white U-shaped brushstrokes. Highlight the slippers along the ankles with white. Paint a white bow under the chin. Paint white dots on nightgown. On the body parts, shade edges with light touches of dark brown.

Paint the plate gold, the candle green, and the flame red. Shade the plate with brown and the candle with dark green. Add pink cheeks, a black wick to the candle, and black facial features.

FINISHING: Drill holes as marked in ornaments; tie on hangers.

PAINTED CAT AND BEAR ORNAMENTS

FOR FRIENDS AND FAMILY

◆ ◆ ◆

There's no greater gift than one made by hand expressing love from the heart. Celebrate the holiday with your family and friends by making and giving these captivating ornaments.

For baby's first Christmas, make the dainty scherenschnitte animal ornaments hanging in the tree, *right.* Choose from a pony, elephant, or sheep design. Cut the shapes from parchment using a sharp scissors or crafts knife. After the cutting is complete, dye your ornament with a strong tea solution. Combine these ornaments in a sweet mobile to hang above baby's crib.

Scherenschnitte, or cutting paper into delicate designs, has been a popular folk-art technique throughout the world for centuries. German immigrants to Pennsylvania brought this paper-cutting tradition with them to the New World. During the 18th and 19th centuries, other

Americans, enamored by these filigree paper creations, began imitating and adapting the technique.

The four ornaments made of baked modeling compound, *right,* will be hung lovingly on the tree each Christmas. The easy-bake girl and boy are formed piece by piece atop a cookie sheet and baked about 10 minutes. Paint the facial details and the recipient's name with acrylic paint, and spray the finished ornament with polyurethane.

Form the parts for Santa and the reindeer separately, then use ribbon to join parts of each ornament together.

Instructions for the easy-bake ornaments are on pages 56–60. Directions for the cut-paper animals are on page 56.

Y ou'll strike a harmonious chord with musical family members and friends when you present them the gift of painted wooden musical instruments, *opposite.*

Make the clever, yet elegant cut-paper cards, *right* and *above,* to send to friends. When each recipient opens the envelope he or she will be surprised to find that the card folds out into a wonderful three-dimensional ornament.

Instructions for these ornaments are on pages 60–66.

These festive knitted keepsakes, featuring a French horn, candle and holly, and a trimmed Christmas tree, can store more than sugary Christmas confections. They'll become diminutive souvenirs of a joy-filled Christmas get-together. Surprise and delight your Christmas dinner guests or holiday visitors by inviting them to choose a treat bag from your tree.

Next year, when these gift ornaments are filled with goodies and hung on your guests' evergreens, they'll bring back memories of special friends and good times spent together.

Knit in stockinette stitch using sport-weight yarn, the bags are made from two knitted squares. An eyelet row of knitting at the top of each square creates openings for weaving narrow ribbons that then are tied into bows. With needle and yarn, the holiday designs are stitched onto the knitted bags using duplicate stitches. Then the two matching squares are sewn together along the bottom and the sides.

Instructions for the knitted treat bags begin on page 66.

Scherenschnitte Animal Ornaments

Shown on pages 50 and 51.

The ornaments measure approximately 3½ inches high.

MATERIALS
White parchment paper
Tracing paper
Graphite paper
Scissors; crafts knife
Gold metallic thread
Tea bags (to dye ornaments)
Paper towels
Cutting surface
Heavy book (to press damp
    ornaments)

INSTRUCTIONS
Trace the full-size patterns, *right*, onto tracing paper. Place graphite paper facedown on parchment paper, then place traced pattern atop graphite paper. Draw over the traced lines to transfer the designs to the parchment.

Place parchment atop a cutting surface. Using the crafts knife, cut out all the dark areas on the inside of the designs.

Cut around the outside of the design using sharp scissors.

Make a strong tea solution; with a paper towel, dab tea onto cut ornaments to antique them. Place dyed ornaments between paper towels and place them between the pages of the heavy book to dry.

Cut a 10-inch length of gold metallic thread for each hanger. Thread the gold thread through the round hole at the back of each animal's head; tie thread into a knot to make a loop.

Easy-Bake Ornaments

Shown on pages 50 and 51.

The girl and boy ornaments measure 3½ inches high; the Santa ornament measures 6 inches high; the reindeer ornament measures 5½ inches high.

SCHERENSCHNITTE
ANIMAL ORNAMENTS

MATERIALS

For the girl
Cernit modeling compound (available at art and crafts stores) in the following colors: white, flesh, yellow, pink, blue-gray, and brown
Acrylic paint in red, black, and white

For the boy
Cernit modeling compound in the following colors: white, flesh, yellow, blue-gray, and orange
Acrylic paint in red, black, and white

For the Santa
Cernit modeling compound in the following colors: red, white, flesh, yellow, green, and black
Acrylic paint in red and black
12 inches of 1/8-inch-wide white satin ribbon (hanger)
12 inches of 1/16-inch-wide white satin ribbon for joining arms and legs
Two small jingle bells
One small white pom-pom
Tracing paper
White crafts glue

For the reindeer
Cernit modeling compound in the following colors: brown, red, white, green, and black
Black acrylic paint
3/4 yard of 1/8-inch red satin ribbon for the hanger and joining legs to body
One tiny brass bell
Tracing paper
White crafts glue

For all ornaments
Liner brush
Polyurethane spray
Garlic press for the hair
Paper clips for hangers
Rolling pin (optional)
Knife; toothpicks
Aluminum foil; baking sheet
Wire cutters

INSTRUCTIONS

Knead all colors of Cernit before forming parts for each ornament. Cover the baking sheet with aluminum foil. Referring to the patterns on page 58 and the photo on pages 50 and 51, form the ornament parts on the aluminum foil.

Bake in a 200-degree oven for 5 to 10 minutes. Ornament will be soft when it's removed from the oven, but will harden as it cools.

When pieces are cool, paint the ornaments.

Spray ornaments with two coats of polyurethane, allowing pieces to dry between coats.

For the girl
To form the robe, use the rolling pin or press a piece of pink Cernit flat; cut a triangle that is about 2¼ inches high and 1½ inches wide at the bottom. Referring to Diagram 1, *bottom, left* on page 58, use the knife to score vertical gather lines.

For robe trims, make a thin roll of blue-gray Cernit. Lay a piece horizontally across waistline. Form two loops and two ties; place at center of waist. Make three tiny balls of blue-gray for buttons; press buttons into place above bow.

Form two 1½-inch-long tapered rolls for arms. Press to the shoulders. The arms will be folded later.

Roll two ½-inch-diameter blue-gray balls for slippers; press to bottom of robe. Press a small amount of blue-gray Cernit through the garlic press; cut off ¼-inch lengths with a toothpick and press to the slippers for fur. Clean the press.

Make two tiny pink spaghetti-like bows and press on the top of the slippers.

From flesh Cernit, form a ¾-inch-diameter ball for the head. Make a tiny ball for the nose and press in place. Make two ¼-inch-diameter balls for hands and press to the end of each arm.

Make two thin blue-gray strips and attach to pink arms just above hands.

To make the blanket, form and stretch a long, thin triangle of white Cernit. Lay the blanket along the right side of the body; bend the arm up across the body with the hand almost to the head. Fold the top of the blanket over the arm.

Knead brown and white Cernit together to make light brown for the bear. Make pieces of the bear, referring to Diagram 2, *bottom, center* on page 58, and join together. Lay bear in place along left side of girl's body. Bend girl's arm around bear's body. Make three small balls of white Cernit and press flat onto tips of bear's legs and arm for paws. Make a tiny brown ball and press to bear's face for a nose.

Load the garlic press with yellow Cernit. Squeeze curls from the press and cut off lengths with a toothpick. Press curls on girl's head and down both shoulders for hair.

Make blue-gray bows for the hair as done previously for the slippers; press in place.

Use wire cutters to cut a paper clip in half; push two ends of one half into the top of the head for the hanger.

Use liner brush and white paint to paint the whites of the bear's eyes. Use black to paint pupils of bear's eyes, girl's eyelashes, and name on blanket. Use red to paint girl's yawning mouth.

For the boy
To form the body, roll out a 1½-inch-long chunky triangular shaped piece of flesh Cernit; press slightly flat.

To make pajama bottoms, flatten a ¼-inch-thick layer of blue-gray Cernit and cover bottom of body. Trim edges with knife to cover bottom of flesh triangle as in Diagram 3, *bottom, right* on page 58. Roll two 1-inch-long blue-gray logs for the legs; press in place.

For the pajama top, press a ¼-inch-thick blue-gray triangle over the top half of the body. Curl the bottom of the triangle up to reveal the tummy. Use a toothpick to poke a hole at the center of the tummy for a belly button.

Form a ¾-inch ball of flesh Cernit for the head. Make a tiny ball for the nose and press in place.

continued

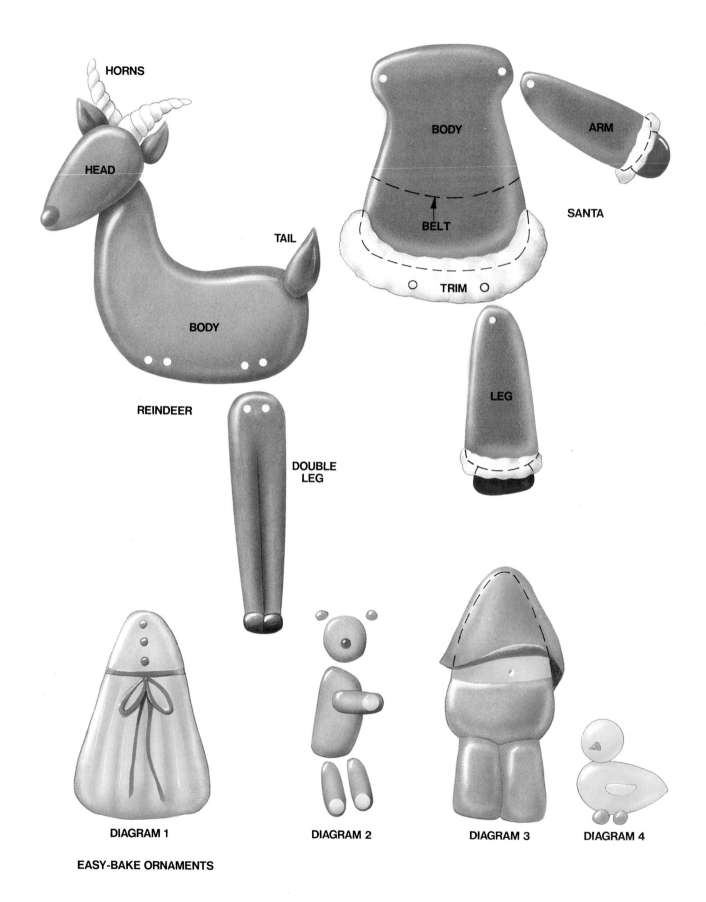

HORNS

HEAD

TAIL

BODY

REINDEER

DOUBLE
LEG

BODY

ARM

SANTA

BELT

TRIM

LEG

DIAGRAM 1

DIAGRAM 2

DIAGRAM 3

DIAGRAM 4

EASY-BAKE ORNAMENTS

To make the pajama neck trim, roll a thin piece of blue-gray Cernit and lay it horizontally between pajama top and head. Use the knife to make some vertical ribbing marks in the neck trim.

Form two 1½-inch-long tapered blue-gray logs for arms. Press to the shoulders. Bend the right arm up toward the head. Leave the other arm alone to position later.

Make two ¼-inch flesh color balls for hands and press one to the end of each arm. Make two ½-inch balls for feet and press to the bottom of each pajama leg.

To make the blanket, form and stretch a long thin triangle of white Cernit. Lay the blanket along the left side and up over the shoulder; bend left arm across the body to hold the blanket.

Load the garlic press with yellow Cernit. Squeeze "hair" curls from the press and cut off ¼-inch lengths with a toothpick. Press hair to top of boy's head.

Referring to Diagram 4, *opposite,* make the duck by rolling a ¾-inch yellow teardrop shape for the body. Press duck body against boy's right leg. Roll a ½-inch ball for the duck's head, and cut a ¼-inch oval for the wing. Make the duck's bill from a tiny orange triangle; press in place. Roll two tiny orange balls for the duck's feet and press in place on the duck's body.

Use wire cutters to cut paper clip in half; push both ends of one half into top of boy's head for the hanger.

Use liner brush and white paint to paint white stitching lines on pajamas. Use black to paint duck's eyes, eyelashes on boy, and name on blanket. Use red to paint the boy's yawning mouth.

For the Santa

Trace body, arm, and leg pattern, *opposite, top,* onto tracing paper.

To make the body parts, use rolling pin or your hand to press out a ball of red clay to ¼-inch thickness. Draw around body, leg, and arm patterns; cut out one body, two arms, and two legs along drawn lines.

To make the belt, roll out a thin string of black Cernit and press it to the middle of the body following dashed line on pattern; trim excess from sides. Layer a small yellow rectangle, a smaller black rectangle, and a tiny yellow oval over the center of the belt for the buckle.

Roll two 1-inch-wide black ovals for the boots. Press ovals against bottom of legs. Flatten the bottoms of the ovals slightly with a knife.

Roll two ½-inch green balls and press one against the end of each arm for mittens.

Roll a ¾-inch ball from flesh for the head; press it against the top of the body and flatten the top slightly.

To make the hat, form a log of red clay. Lay it over the top of the head and curl it up on one side; flatten slightly.

To make the fur trim for the hat and cuffs, roll white Cernit into a narrow log shape and flatten to about ¼ inch wide. Press hat and cuff trims in place, overlapping the wrists and mittens, and the face and hat; trim excess. For the bottom of the coat make a ½-inch-wide trim. Place coat trim along edge of red body; trim excess. Texture fur trim with a toothpick point.

Push white Cernit through the garlic press and cut off ¼-inch lengths; layer along sides of head and forehead for hair and beard. Fill in beard area with more pressed Cernit. Make tiny strand of white clay for the mustache. Place strand onto head, curving tips of mustache up. Make a red ball nose and place it above the mustache. Poke a hole below the mustache with a toothpick for the mouth.

Make a candy cane by twisting a thin strand of red Cernit and a thin strand of white Cernit together. Cut candy cane to 1½ inches long, curve tip, and lay across one of Santa's hands.

For the other hand, make a gift using a ¾-inch square of yellow Cernit for the box. Add two thin green Cernit strings for the ribbon and add a bow shape, referring to instructions for the girl ornament. Lay the gift across the hand.

Using a toothpick, pierce ⅛-inch holes on the tops of each arm and leg and four holes on the body, as marked on the Santa patterns.

Use wire cutters to cut paper clip in half; push the ends of one half into top of the Santa's head for the hanger.

Use liner brush and white paint to paint whites of eyes. Use black to paint irises, eye outline, and lashes.

ASSEMBLY: Cut four 6-inch lengths of 1/16-inch-wide ribbon. Thread ribbons through each shoulder and arm; thread ribbons through each leg and bottom of coat trim. Tie tiny bows and trim excess. Touch knot in center of each bow with white crafts glue; allow to dry.

Glue pom-pom to curled tip of hat.

Thread ⅛-inch ribbon through paper clip hanger; tie a jingle bell on each side of ribbon and tie an overhand knot at top of ribbon to form loop.

For the reindeer

Trace body and double leg pattern onto tracing paper, *opposite.*

To make the reindeer, knead and mix the brown and white Cernit together. Use the rolling pin or your hand to press the Cernit to ¼-inch thickness. Draw around body and double leg patterns. Using a knife, cut along lines to make one body and two double legs; round cut edges to give them a softer look.

Roll a 1-inch teardrop shape for the head and press it to the top of the body at the neck. Form a small red ball and attach it to the end of the face for a nose.

continued

Make the two ears and the tail by forming three ¼-inch-long teardrop shapes. Use the knife to press a vertical indentation in the center of each ear and the tail. Place the ears and tail as shown on page 58.

To make the horns, roll two 1-inch-long white strands; twist each horn, making a spiral texture. Join them behind each ear.

Make two ½-inch black ovals for the hooves; place them on the bottom of the double leg sections. Use the knife to cut a crease down the middle of each double leg section and hoof.

Push green clay through a garlic press; cut off ¼-inch lengths and layer around the neck of the reindeer to form a wreath. Continue to add layers until the wreath is full. Roll tiny red clay berries and place throughout the wreath.

Use wire cutters to cut the paper clip in half; push the ends of one half into the top of the reindeer's head for the hanger.

Using a toothpick, pierce ⅛-inch holes on the tops of the legs and bottom of body as marked on the patterns.

Use liner brush and black paint for the eyelashes.

ASSEMBLY: Cut two 6-inch lengths of ⅛-inch-wide ribbon. Thread each ribbon through two holes in one side of bottom of body. Lay double leg section over body and thread ribbon through both holes; tie a bow and trim excess ribbon tails. Repeat for the other leg section. Tie a tiny bow and glue it to the wreath; glue bell below bow. Dab glue on knots of all bows to keep them closed. Cut a 12-inch length of ribbon and thread it through the paper clip hanger; tie ribbon into a loop.

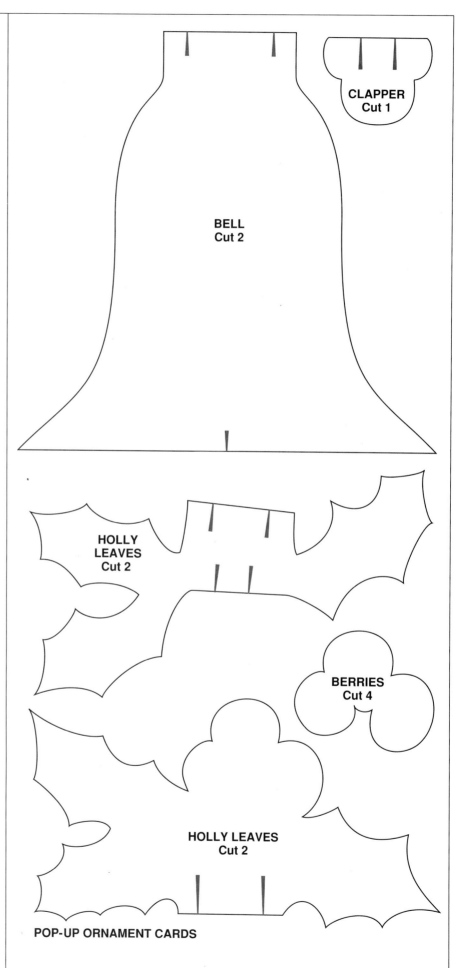

CLAPPER
Cut 1

BELL
Cut 2

HOLLY
LEAVES
Cut 2

BERRIES
Cut 4

HOLLY LEAVES
Cut 2

POP-UP ORNAMENT CARDS

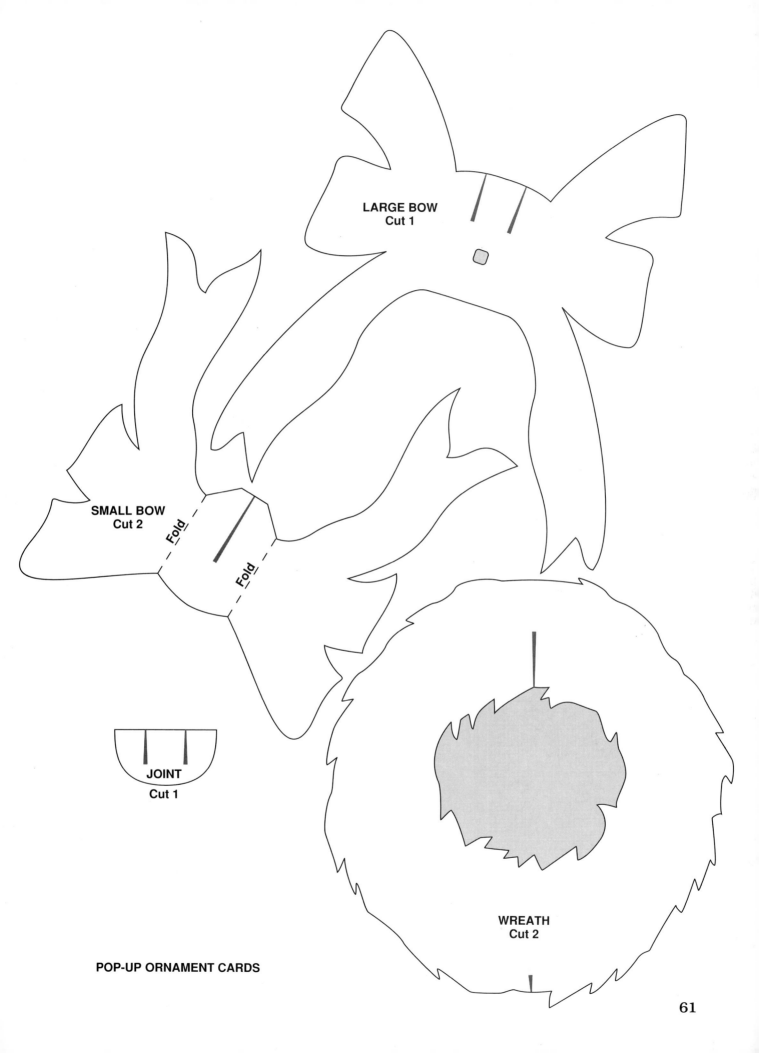

LARGE BOW
Cut 1

SMALL BOW
Cut 2

Fold

Fold

JOINT
Cut 1

WREATH
Cut 2

POP-UP ORNAMENT CARDS

61

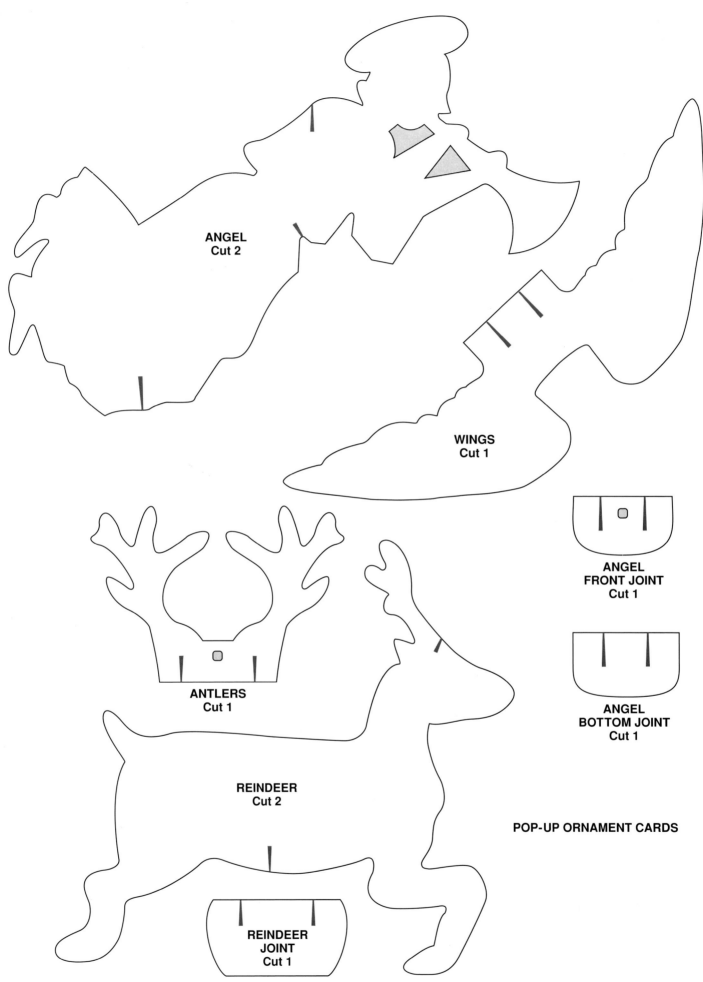

ANGEL
Cut 2

WINGS
Cut 1

ANGEL
FRONT JOINT
Cut 1

ANGEL
BOTTOM JOINT
Cut 1

ANTLERS
Cut 1

REINDEER
Cut 2

POP-UP ORNAMENT CARDS

REINDEER
JOINT
Cut 1

Pop-up Ornament Cards

Shown on page 53.

Each ornament fits into a 5x7-inch envelope.

MATERIALS
For bell ornament
130-lb. watercolor paper
8½x11-inch piece of medium-weight green paper
Scrap of red metallic wrapping paper
Sharp embroidery or manicure scissors

For wreath ornament
Red and green medium weight paper

For angel ornament
130-lb. watercolor paper

For reindeer ornament
130-lb. watercolor paper

For all ornaments
Tracing paper
Graphite paper
Kneaded eraser; pencil
Crafts knife; extra blades
Scissors
Glue stick
10 inches of ⅛-inch-wide ribbon or gold cord for each ornament hanger

INSTRUCTIONS
Trace the full-size patterns, *opposite* and on pages 60 and 61 onto tracing paper. Place graphite paper facedown on watercolor or colored paper; place tracing paper on top of graphite paper. Draw over traced lines with a sharp pencil.

Cut the number of pieces given on the pattern using a sharp scissors or crafts knife. Change knife blades often for clean cutting. Cut narrow slits in pieces where indicated by blue lines on the patterns. After cutting, gently erase any of the remaining graphite lines.

To use an ornament as a card, assemble the card and write your message. Do not fold; mail in a purchased 5x7-inch envelope.

continued

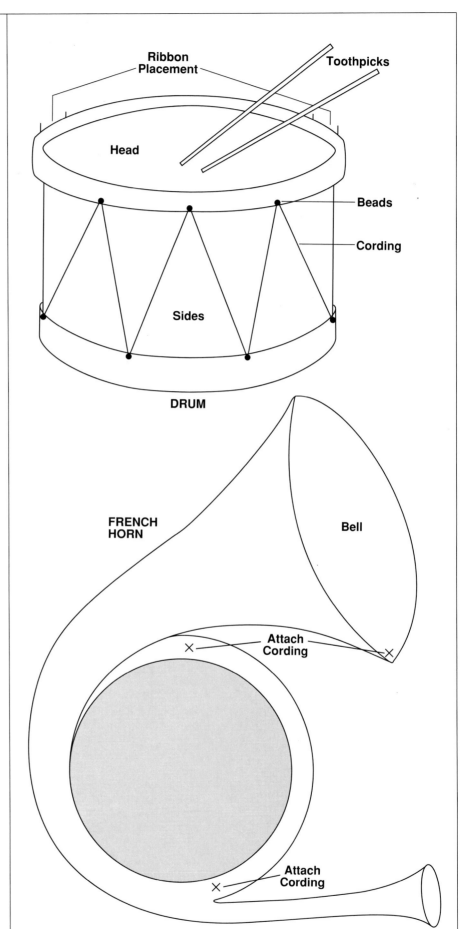

MUSICAL INSTRUMENT ORNAMENTS

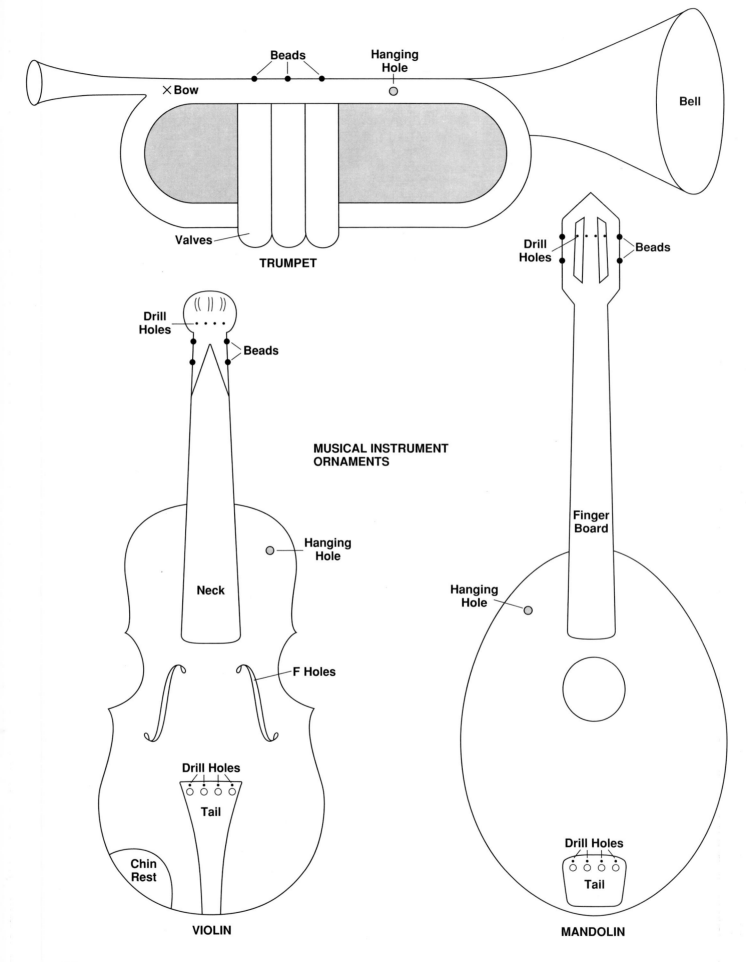

Beads   Hanging Hole

×Bow

Valves

TRUMPET

Bell

Drill Holes   Beads

Drill Holes   Beads

MUSICAL INSTRUMENT ORNAMENTS

Hanging Hole

Finger Board

Neck

Hanging Hole

F Holes

Drill Holes

Tail

Chin Rest

VIOLIN

Drill Holes

Tail

MANDOLIN

To hang, place pieces at right angles to each other to give ornament dimension.

For the bell ornament

For the bell, clapper, and two holly pieces, use the full-size patterns on page 60.

Cut two bell shapes and one clapper from watercolor paper. Cut two of each holly piece from green paper. Cut four berry pieces from red metallic paper.

Glue red metallic berries to both sides of the holly leaf pieces with berry shapes at the top.

Insert slits of the two plain holly pieces into matching slits in tops of the bell pieces. The holly pieces will be perpendicular to the bell pieces.

Insert slits of the two holly pieces with berries into matching slits of plain holly pieces. These berry pieces will be perpendicular to the plain holly pieces.

Insert slits of the clapper into matching slits at the bottom of the bell pieces. The clapper piece will be perpendicular to the two bell pieces.

Run a 10-inch length of ribbon or gold cording through the center of the two bells below the two holly pieces; tie overhand knot in cord to make a loop for hanging.

For the wreath ornament

For the wreath, two bows, and joint, use the full-size patterns on page 61.

Cut two wreaths and one joint from green paper. Cut two small bow pieces and one large bow piece from red paper. Cut away the shaded area in the wreath. Cut hole in large bow for hanger.

Insert slits of the large bow into long matching slits at the inner tops of the two wreaths. The bow will be perpendicular to the wreaths.

Insert the slit of each small bow down into the slits on the large bow. The small bows will lie flat against the wreath. Fold the small bows outward along fold lines on the pattern.

Insert slits of the joint into matching slits at the bottom of wreaths. The joint will be perpendicular to the wreath.

Run a 10-inch length of ribbon or cording through hole in center of large bow; tie overhand knot in cord to make a loop for hanging.

For the angel ornament

For the angel, wings, and two joints, use the full-size patterns on page 62.

Cut two angel pieces, one wing piece, and one each of front and bottom joints from watercolor paper. Cut out shaded areas on the angel.

Run a 10-inch length of ribbon or gold cording through the hole of the front joint; tie an overhand knot in the cord to make a loop.

Insert the slits of the front joint into matching slits at the waist of the two angels. The joint will be perpendicular to the angels.

Insert slits of the bottom joint into matching slits in the bottom of the two angel pieces. This joint will be perpendicular to angels.

Insert the slits of the wings into the matching slits at the top of the angel pieces. The wings will be perpendicular to the angels.

For reindeer ornament

For reindeer, joint, and antlers, use full-size patterns on page 62.

Cut two reindeer pieces, one antler piece, and one joint from watercolor paper. Cut hole in antler for hanger.

Run a 10-inch length of ribbon or gold cording through the hole of the antler piece; tie overhand knot in cord to make loop.

Insert slits of the antlers into matching slits in the heads of the reindeer. This joint will be perpendicular to the reindeer.

Insert the slits of the joint into the matching slits in the bottom of the reindeer. This joint will be perpendicular to the reindeer.

Musical Instrument Ornaments

Shown on page 52.

The violin is 6½ inches long, the mandolin and trumpet are 7½ inches long, the French horn is 4½x5½ inches long, and the drum is 3 inches high.

MATERIALS

8x12-inch piece of ¼-inch Baltic birch plywood
Tracing paper
Delta Ceramcoat paints in the following colors: Burnt Sienna, Brown Velvet, Raw Sienna, Golden Brown, Midnight, Nightfall, Blue Danube, Sandstone, Black, Spice Tan, Antique Gold, Sunbright Yellow, Maple Sugar, Ivory, and White
Matte finish water-base varnish
Assorted artist's paintbrushes
Mop brush
3-mm red cording for the drum
8-mm red cording for the horn
1 yard of red grosgrain ribbon
Fabric stiffening and draping solution
Gold metallic thread; needle
Two toothpicks; gold spray paint
Three 6-mm gold beads
Seven 2-mm gold beads
Eight 2-mm black wooden beads
White crafts glue
Sandpaper
Band saw or jigsaw; drill

INSTRUCTIONS

Trace full-size instrument patterns, *opposite* and on page 63 onto tracing paper. Cut out paper patterns. Draw around each of the patterns on the plywood; use a band saw or jigsaw to cut pieces from plywood. Drill small holes as marked on patterns. Sand all pieces. Follow painting instructions for each instrument. After paint has dried, apply matte varnish; then add finishing details.

For the violin

PAINTING: Base-paint both sides of the violin with Burnt Sienna. Shade the outside edges of the violin with Brown Velvet.

Use the mop brush to add highlights of Raw Sienna to the body of the violin.

Paint the chin rest, neck, tail piece, and F holes with Black.

continued

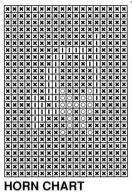 ◄ Eyelet row

HORN CHART

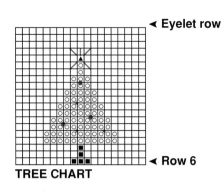 ◄ Eyelet row

◄ Row 6

TREE CHART

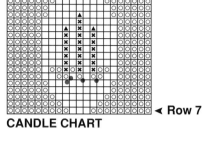 ◄ Eyelet row

◄ Row 7

CANDLE CHART

CANDY BAG ORNAMENTS

COLOR KEY

☒ Vermilion　　◎ Paddy Green　　⊡ Light Gold　　◉ Daffodil French Knot
▲ Daffodil　　　■ Fawn Beige　　☐ Ecru　　　　✦ Vermilion French Knot

Paint the scroll strokes at the top of the neck with Raw Sienna.

Paint dots of Burnt Sienna directly below the drilled holes in the tail piece.

FINISHING: Glue four black beads to the sides of the neck as indicated on the pattern.

Thread the needle with a 24-inch length of gold thread. Beginning behind the tail piece in the back of the violin, bring the needle and thread through the wood to the front of the tail piece, leaving a 3-inch gold thread tail in back. Sew the thread up and down the neck of the violin, through a hole, through the next hole and back down to the bottom; ending in the back of the tail piece. Tie the thread tails together; add a drop of crafts glue to the tails to secure them.

Tie a 10-inch length of gold thread through the hanging hole.

For the drum
PAINTING: Paint both sides of the drum the same, as follows. Stain the top and bottom rims with Golden Brown; shade with Maple Sugar. Paint the sides with Nightfall; paint the head Ivory. Shade the edges of the sides with Midnight. Dry-brush a highlight of Blue Danube across the middle of the sides. Use Sandstone to shade the edges of the drum head.

FINISHING: Glue the red cording up and down along the markings on the drum sides. Glue a 2-mm gold bead at each X.

Spray-paint the two toothpicks gold; when dry, glue to drum head.

Cut a 13-inch length of red ribbon and coat it in stiffening solution; wipe off excess. Lay ribbon out on wax paper to dry, arranging it in a curved shape as it dries. Glue ribbon ends to back of drum, as indicated on the pattern. Hang from ribbon.

For the mandolin
PAINTING: Base-coat the front and back of the mandolin with Maple Sugar. Paint the finger board, back, sides, and tail piece with Brown Velvet. Paint the hole Black. Paint the strokes on the decorative bands around the outside edge and around the center hole with Brown Velvet. Use Black to paint the dots below the drilled holes in the tail. Use Brown Velvet to add shading next to the finger board and tail.

FINISHING: Follow the finishing instructions given for the violin.

For the French horn and the trumpet
PAINTING: Base-coat both the horn and trumpet with Antique Gold. Shade around all edges and lines on the patterns with An-

tique Brown. Brush highlights on the mouthpieces, bell rims, and center of the metal tubing with Sunbright Yellow. Mix Sunbright Yellow and White; dry-brush added highlights along the curves of the bell and metal tubing.

FINISHING: For the French horn, tie an overhand knot 1 inch from each end of the 8-mm cording; unravel the ends. Glue cording at each X on the pattern, with the knots attached to the tubing. Hang horn from the red cording.

For the trumpet, make a bow with the remaining red grosgrain ribbon; glue in position near the mouthpiece on the trumpet. Glue three 6-mm gold beads above the three valves.

Insert an 8-inch length of gold metallic thread in the drilled hanging hole; tie into a loop.

Candy Bag Ornaments

Shown on pages 54 and 55.

The French horn bag and the Christmas tree bag measure approximately 2¾x3¾ inches; the candle bag measures 3x4 inches.

MATERIALS

For the French horn bag

Coats & Clark Red Heart Super Sport yarn (3-ounce skein): 1 skein each of vermilion (918), paddy green (687), and light gold (605)
Size 5 knitting needles

For the Christmas tree bag

Coats & Clark Red Heart Super Sport yarn (3-ounce skein): 1 skein each of paddy green (687), vermilion (918), fawn beige (322), and daffodil (225)
Size 5 knitting needles
Three bobbins

For the candle bag

Coats & Clark Red Heart Super Sport yarn (3-ounce skein): 1 skein each of paddy green (687), ecru (109), vermilion (918), and daffodil (225)
Size 4 knitting needles
Three bobbins

For all bags

Tapestry needle
10 inches of ¼-inch-wide ribbon per bag
8 inches of gold metallic thread for each hanger

Abbreviations: See page 73.
Gauge: 6 sts = 1 inch in st st on Size 4 needles; 5½ sts = 1 inch in st st on Size 5 needles.

INSTRUCTIONS

For the French horn bag

(Make 2): With Size 5 needles and vermilion, cast on 18 sts. Beginning with a purl row, work 25 rows of st st.
Eyelet row: K 1, * k 2 tog, yo, * rep from * to last st; k 1.
Work 5 more rows in st st; bind off sts.

DUPLICATE STITCHING: Refer to the duplicate stitch diagram, *right*, for stitching sequence to work the duplicate stitches. Following the Horn Chart, *opposite*, duplicate st the horn on the front of the bag using the tapestry needle and light gold; duplicate st the ribbon with paddy green.

FINISHING: Place the bag halves together, wrong sides together, and sew side and bottom seams of bag together. Weave in yarn ends.
Thread the ribbon through the eyelet row and tie into a bow.
Sew gold thread through the top back of bag; tie into loop.

For the Christmas tree bag

BAG BACK (make 1): With Size 5 needles and ecru, cast on 19 sts. Beginning with a purl row, work 25 rows of st st; dec 1 st on last row—24 sts.
Eyelet row: K 1, * k 2 tog, yo, * rep from * to last st; k 1.
Work 5 more rows of st st; bind off sts.

BAG FRONT (make 1): *Note:* Use one bobbin of paddy green to work tree and two bobbins of ecru to work background. After the bag front is knitted, the tree stand, trunk, star, and ornaments are worked in duplicate stitch.
Cast on 19 sts with ecru. Beginning with a purl row, work 5 rows of st st.
Next row: Continuing in st st, begin Tree Chart, *top center, opposite*, using bobbins to work design. Complete chart; dec 1 st on last row of chart. Work eyelet row as for Bag Back. Bind off sts.

DUPLICATE STITCHING: Referring to the Tree Chart, use the tapestry needle to duplicate st the tree stand with vermilion, the trunk with fawn beige, and the star with daffodil. Work straight stitches of daffodil out from the star. Refer to the diagram, *bottom, right*, to work straight stitches. Work French knots of vermilion and daffodil for the ball ornaments. To work French knots, see the diagram, *right*. Refer to the finishing instructions for the French horn to complete bag.

For the candle bag

BAG BACK (make 1): With Size 4 needles and paddy green, cast on 21 sts. Beginning with a purl row, work 29 rows of st st.
Eyelet row: K 1, * k 2 tog, yo, * rep from * to last 2 sts; k 2.
Work 5 more rows of st st; bind off sts.

BAG FRONT (make 1): *Note:* Use a bobbin of ecru to work the circle and two bobbins of paddy green to work background. After the bag front is knitted, the candles, holly, and berries are worked in duplicate stitch.
Cast on 21 sts in paddy green. Beginning with a purl row, work 5 rows st st. *Next row:* Continuing in st st, begin Candle Chart, *top right, opposite*, using bobbins to work the ecru circle design. Complete the chart. Work 4 more rows of paddy green in st st, then work eyelet row as for Bag Back. Bind off sts.

DUPLICATE STITCHING: Referring to the Candle Chart, use the tapestry needle to duplicate st the holly with paddy green, the candles with vermilion, and the candle flames with daffodil. Work French knots of vermilion for the holly berries. Refer to the finishing instructions for the French horn to complete the bag.

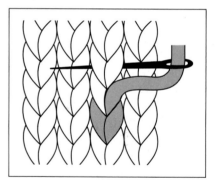

DUPLICATE STITCH

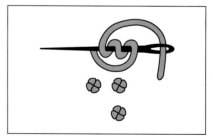

FRENCH KNOT

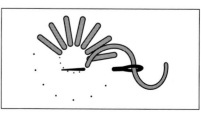

STRAIGHT STITCH

HANDCRAFTED WITH LOVE

A COUNTRY SAMPLING

No matter where you live—a white, frame farmhouse nestled in America's heartland or a steel and glass high-rise apartment piercing an urban skyline—your address will have that cozy "country" feel this Christmas when it's decorated with the crafts presented here.

Create a miniature quilt pillow as a tree ornament or package trim using the eight cross-stitch quilt block designs on page 72. Duplicate the ornaments on the tree, *left,* or stitch the designs in any combination you choose. Hand-sew a second square of Aida cloth to the first and lightly stuff your pillow. Softly fray the edges and hang the ornament with a cord.

Recall the inventive crazy quilts of yesteryear by recycling old knit scraps to make the colorful heart-shaped tokens of love,

left. You may wish to give your knit-remnant hearts a crazy-quilt feel by embellishing them with your favorite embroidery stitches. Sew a special button in the center of the heart.

Make the cute country angels, *left,* with felt. Coat them with gesso and paint them with acrylic paints. Dress them in calico, gingham, and check dresses. Glue on halos of eucalyptus leaves and red lacquered berries. Add Spanish moss collars to the dresses for a natural country touch.

Instructions for the three projects are on pages 72–74.

Stiffened felt, modeling paste, acrylic paint, and raw wool create the jolly cone-shaped Santa, *opposite*.

Cut the jointed Santa, angel, and rooster ornaments, *above,* from balsa wood using a crafts knife or, for sturdier ornaments, cut all of these painted wood designs from hardboard using a jigsaw.

Instructions for these ornaments are on pages 75–79.

Cross-Stitch Quilt Design Ornaments

Shown on pages 68 and 69.

The finished ornaments measure 4 inches square.

MATERIALS
For one ornament
Two 8-inch squares of 14-count Aida cloth (We used Wheatstraw from Charles Craft.)
One skein each of DMC embroidery floss in colors listed on the color key
Tapestry needle
Sewing thread to match Aida cloth
Fiberfill; white paper tape
8-inch length of gold metallic thread

INSTRUCTIONS
Use two strands of the floss to work cross-stitches over one square of the Aida cloth. Refer to page 44 for diagram on working cross-stitches.

Work one cross-stitch for each symbol on the chart, *above right.* Hem or tape the raw edges of the fabric to prevent the threads from raveling.

Locate the center of one piece of Aida cloth and the center of the Border pattern, *right;* begin stitching here. Using the designs on the chart, cross-stitch a quilt block design in each of the four squares. Refer to the photograph on pages 68 and 69, for ideas on combinations of the quilt square designs.

When cross-stitching is completed, remove the tape. With wrong sides together, sew the second square of Aida cloth to the stitched square, sewing two fabric squares beyond the stitched border (see the stitching line on the pattern); leave an opening for stuffing. Stuff lightly; sew the opening closed. Trim around the ornament to within 6 squares of the sewing line. Gently unravel the outside threads of the fabric to one square beyond the sewing line.

Sew a gold metallic thread through a side or corner of the ornament; tie into a loop.

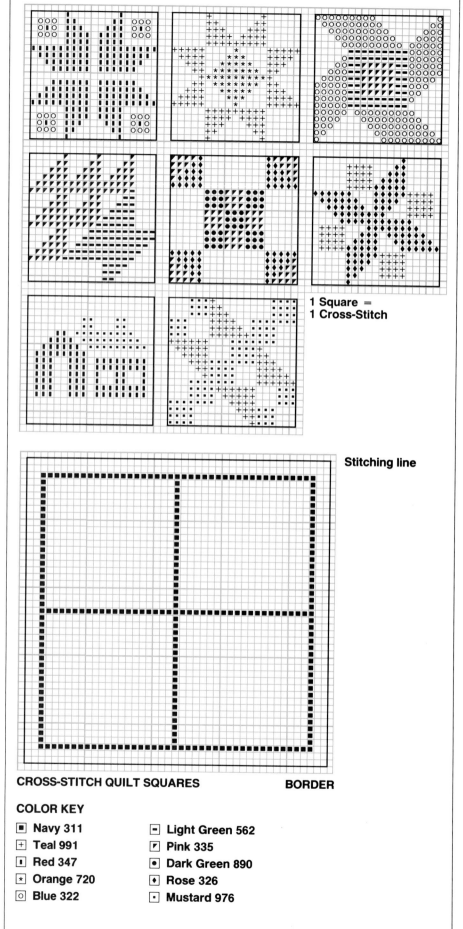

1 Square = 1 Cross-Stitch

Stitching line

CROSS-STITCH QUILT SQUARES   BORDER

COLOR KEY

▣	Navy 311	⊟	Light Green 562
⊞	Teal 991	◪	Pink 335
▮	Red 347	⊡	Dark Green 890
★	Orange 720	◈	Rose 326
⊙	Blue 322	⊡	Mustard 976

Sweater-Knit Heart Ornament

Shown on pages 68 and 69.

Heart measures 4¾ inches across at the widest part.

MATERIALS
For one ornament
Two 5½-inch squares of knit sock or old sweater fabric
Two 5½-inch squares of fusible interfacing
Tracing paper
Polyester fiberfill
Assorted colors of embroidery floss
Two buttons
Doll needle
Sewing thread
10-inch length of gold metallic thread

INSTRUCTIONS
Fold tracing paper in half. Lay tracing paper atop heart pattern, *right*, aligning fold of paper with the dashed fold line on the pattern. Trace the full-size heart pattern, onto tracing paper. Cut out the pattern, completing the heart shape.

Fuse the interfacing to the wrong sides of both squares of knit fabric following the manufacturer's instructions.

With the knit stitches running up and down, draw around the heart shape on the interfaced side of one of the knit fabric squares. With right sides together, pin the second square of knit fabric to the first. Sew along the drawn line, leaving an opening on one side of the heart for turning as indicated on the pattern. Cut out the heart allowing for a ¼-inch seam allowance. Clip curves and turn the heart right side out; stuff firmly with fiberfill and slip-stitch the opening closed.

If desired, use six strands of embroidery floss to embellish both sides of the heart with embroidery stitches, such as French knots, lazy daisy stitches, running stitches, chain stitches, and cross-stitches. Refer to the stitch diagrams, *right* and on pages 44 and 67 to work the embroidery stitches. Refer to the photograph on pages 68 and 69 for some stitching ideas.

Using the doll needle, sew a button in the center of both sides of the heart. Stitch through one button, through the heart, and through the button on the opposite side. Pull the sewing thread tight to give the heart its shape. Continue sewing through both buttons until they are secure.

Sew the gold metallic thread through the top center of the heart. Tie thread into a loop for the hanger.

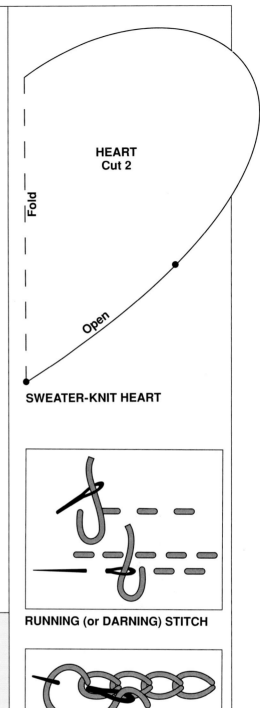

**HEART
Cut 2**

Fold

Open

SWEATER-KNIT HEART

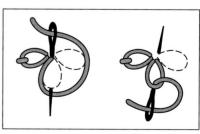

RUNNING (or DARNING) STITCH

CHAIN STITCH

LAZY DAISY STITCH

Knitting and Crocheting Abbreviations

beg	begin(ning)	rep	repeat
CC	contrasting color	RH	right hand
ch	chain	rnd(s)	round(s)
dc	double crochet	sc	single crochet
dec	decrease	sk	skip
grp	group	sl	slip
hdc	half-double crochet	sl st	slip stitch
inc	increase	sp	space
k	knit	st(s)	stitch(es)
LH	left hand	st st	stockinette stitch
lp(s)	loop(s)	tbl	through back loop
MC	main color	tog	together
p	purl	trc	treble crochet
pat(s)	pattern(s)	yo	yarn over
psso	pass sl st over	*	repeat from * as indicated
rem	remaining	( ) repeat between ( ) as indicated	
		[ ] repeat between [ ] as indicated	

Country Angel Ornament

Shown on pages 68 and 69.

Angel measures 4 inches high.

MATERIALS
For one ornament
6x12-inch piece of black felt for body and wings

2¼x12-inch strip of country print fabric for dress

Tracing paper

Fiberfill

Spanish moss

Small eucalyptus leaves

Two tiny red lacquered berries

Gesso

Water-base antiquing medium

Foam brush; small artist's paintbrush

Acrylic paints in the following colors: flesh, ivory, black, and dark red for the head and wings; red, green, gold, or country blue for the body

10-inch length of gold metallic thread

White fabric marking pencil

Hot-glue gun

INSTRUCTIONS
Note: These patterns include ¼-inch seam allowances. Sew all pieces with right sides together unless otherwise instructed.

BODY: Trace the body and wing patterns, *right*, onto tracing paper; cut out patterns.

Using the white fabric marking pencil, draw around pattern shapes on black felt. Cut one wing piece and two body pieces.

Sew body pieces together, leaving an opening for turning as indicated on the pattern. Clip curves, turn, stuff, and slip-stitch the opening closed.

Use the foam brush to apply gesso to both sides of the wings and body. Allow gesso to dry thoroughly. The gesso stiffens the felt and prepares it for painting.

Paint the head flesh color. Paint the body with a color that complements the dress fabric. Paint the

WINGS
Cut 1

BODY
CUT 2

Open

COUNTRY ANGEL ORNAMENT

wings ivory. Allow the paints to dry. Brush the antiquing medium over the painted pieces. Leave antiquing on about 5 minutes, then wipe off excess. On the face, paint black dots for eyes and a dark red line for the mouth. Mix ivory and dark red paint; using your finger, apply a smudge of the resulting pink to the cheeks.

DRESS: Run a gathering thread along one long side of the dress fabric. Turn under a ¼-inch hem along the other long side of the dress fabric. Sew the hem in place. Stitch the two short sides of the dress fabric together. Slip the dress over the angel. Pull the gathering thread to fit around the neck of the angel. Tie the ends of the gathering thread into a knot behind the angel's head to secure.

FINISHING: Use the hot-glue gun to apply Spanish moss around the neck of the dress. Paint a tiny, dark red heart on the front of the dress just above the hem.

Hot-glue eucalyptus and berries to the top of the head. Glue wings to the back of the angel.

Thread a gold thread through the eucalyptus on top of the head; knot the ends to form a loop for hanging.

Felt Cone-Shaped Santa Ornament

Shown on page 70.

Santa is approximately 6¼ inches high.

MATERIALS
For one ornament
8x11-inch piece of red felt
Scrap of peach felt for the face
Tracing paper
Fabric stiffening and draping solution
Raw wool for the beard
One 7-inch-high plastic-foam cone for shaping Santa
Aluminum foil
Red, black, and white acrylic paints
Fine-tipped artist's paintbrush
½-inch flat artist's paintbrush

Texturing or modeling paste (available at art stores)
Butter spreader to apply texturing paste
Cotton swab
Scrap of gold metallic poster board for the belt buckle
10-inch length of fish line; one paper clip
Sewing needle
Red and peach sewing threads
Plastic bag
Hot-glue gun

INSTRUCTIONS
Trace the body and face patterns on page 76 onto tracing paper. Cut out traced patterns.

Draw around the body pattern atop red felt; cut out body. Draw around face pattern atop peach felt; cut out face.

Sew the face piece to the body as indicated on the pattern by the dashed placement line.

Shape the body into a cone, overlapping the opposite long straight edge over the tab; pin in place. Sew the edges together using a running stitch along the overlapped edge.

Pour stiffening and draping solution into the plastic bag. Place the body in the bag and squeeze the solution completely through the felt. Squeeze out the excess solution.

Cover the plastic foam cone with aluminum foil to keep the felt from sticking to it. Place the body shape over the cone. Remove the body from the cone when dry.

Using the fine-tipped paintbrush, paint the eyes black, the nose line black, the eyebrows white, and the lips red. After the paint has dried, add white highlight to the eyes. Mix a light gray color using black and white paints; add gray to the eyebrows.

Mix red and white together for pink; apply pink to cheeks with the cotton swab.

Using the ½-inch flat brush, paint a black belt around the waist. Allow paint to dry.

Make a loop with the fish line and knot. Place the paper clip onto the loop by the knot. Insert the loop up through inside of body and through the point of the

hat. Hot-glue the paper clip to the inside of the hat point.

For fur, use the butter spreader to apply swirling layers of texturing paste around the bottom of the cone and hat as indicated on the pattern by the texture design. Add texturing paste to the point of the hat, keeping the hanger in the middle.

After the paste has dried completely, mix gray paint; use it to paint the indentations in the textured fur.

For the buckle, cut a ½-inch square from gold metallic poster board. Hot-glue the gold square to the center of the belt.

Hot-glue the raw wool to the face for the beard and mustache.

Painted and Jointed Wood Ornaments

Shown on page 71.

The Santa and rooster are approximately 7 inches high; the angel is 8 inches high.

MATERIALS
For all three ornaments
4x30-inch piece of ⅛-inch-thick balsa wood or tempered hardboard
Red, white, black, brown, yellow, green, and metallic-gold acrylic paints
Assorted artist's paintbrushes
Paper plate or paint palette
Light wood stain; paintbrush
Soft rag; pencil
Crafts knife (for balsa wood) or a jigsaw (for tempered hardboard)
Three brass paper fasteners
Tracing paper; graphite paper
1 yard of gold metallic thread for the hangers
Sandpaper; ⅛-inch drill bit
Drill (for tempered hardboard)
continued

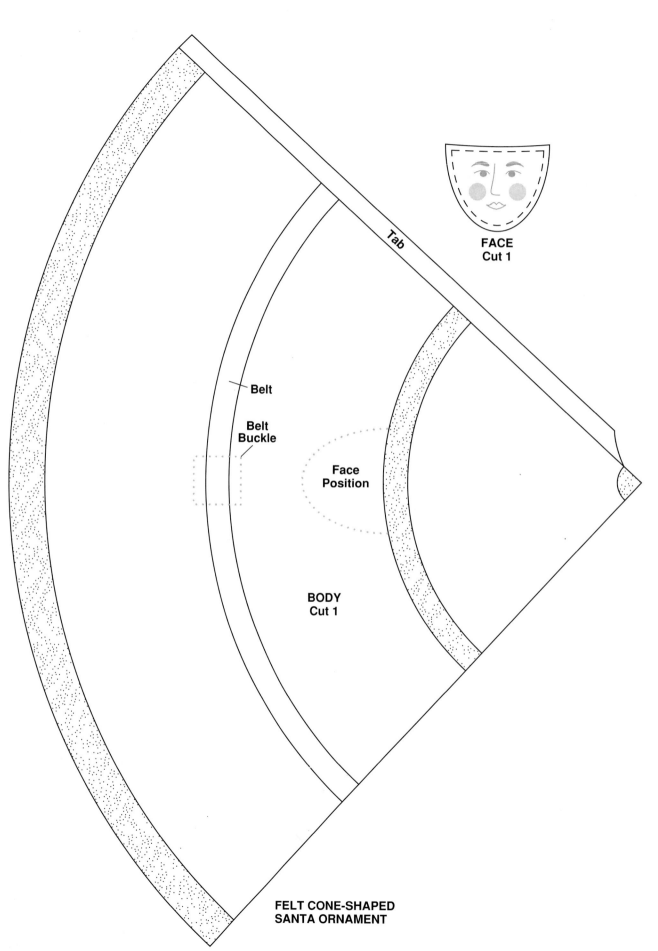

FACE
Cut 1

Tab

Belt

Belt
Buckle

Face
Position

BODY
Cut 1

**FELT CONE-SHAPED
SANTA ORNAMENT**

INSTRUCTIONS

Note: If you use balsa wood, the only tools you'll need are a crafts knife and a drill bit. The balsa wood ornaments will be fragile. If you have a jigsaw, you can cut the ornaments from tempered hardboard. You'll also need a drill if you use hardboard.

CUTTING: Trace the patterns, *right* and on page 78, onto tracing paper. Lay graphite paper on top of balsa or tempered hardboard; place the traced patterns atop the graphite paper. Transfer the designs to the wood using a pencil to trace the design lines. Cut pieces from wood using either a crafts knife or jigsaw.

Lightly sand the wood before painting.

PAINTING: Use the photograph on page 71 as a guide while painting. Paint the angel's dress white, her hair brown, and her wings yellow. Outline and shade the angel's wings with metallic-gold paint; add tiny dots of gold paint to the hem of her dress. Paint Santa's suit red, his fur white, and his mittens, boots, and belt black. Paint the rooster's body white, its wings black, and its legs yellow.

Refer to the photograph to complete detail painting.

Brush light wood stain over all ornament parts, then wipe stain away, leaving just enough to antique the surfaces.

ASSEMBLY: Using the drill bit, poke holes into the balsa wood where indicated on the patterns. (Drill holes into tempered hardboard ornaments.) To join each arm and leg to a body, insert a brass fastener into the arm or leg hole, then into the body; open the fastener.

Add a gold thread hanger to the hole at the top of each ornament.

Painted Folk-Art Santas

Shown on page 71.

Santas measure 4½, 5, and 6 inches high.

MATERIALS
For three ornaments
7x12-inch piece of ⅛- or ¼-inch-thick tempered hardboard
Tracing paper; graphite paper
Ballpoint pen; sandpaper
Acrylic paints in the following colors: red, blue, green, white, black, and flesh
Assorted artist's paintbrushes
Paint palette
White primer; sponge brush
Water-base varnish
Jigsaw; drill; ⅛-inch drill bit
1 yard of gold metallic cording

INSTRUCTIONS
Trace the full-size patterns on page 79 onto tracing paper. With graphite paper sandwiched between wood and the traced patterns, transfer the designs to hardboard with the ballpoint pen.

Cut out wood ornaments using the jigsaw. Sand all surfaces and prime with white paint; sand the primed surface.

PAINTING: Refer to the photographs of each Santa on page 71 as you paint details.

For the wizard Santa, use flesh color to paint the star on the staff, the moon, and face. Paint the mittens red, the fur trims and beard white, and the clothing blue. Use black to paint the stars along the fur on bottom of clothing, the eyes, and the staff. Outline arms with flesh color.

continued

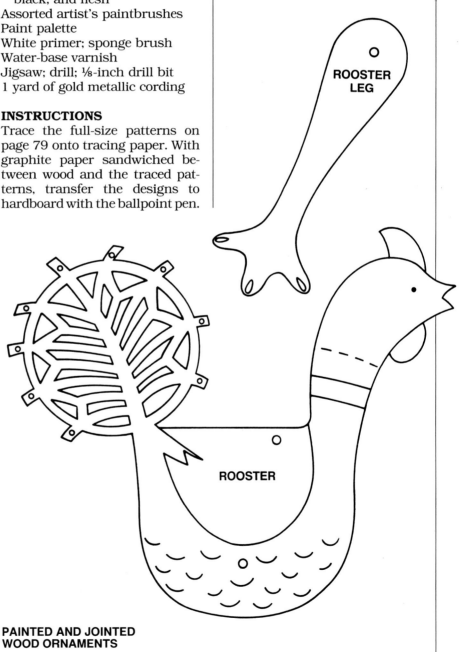

ROOSTER LEG

ROOSTER

PAINTED AND JOINTED WOOD ORNAMENTS

77

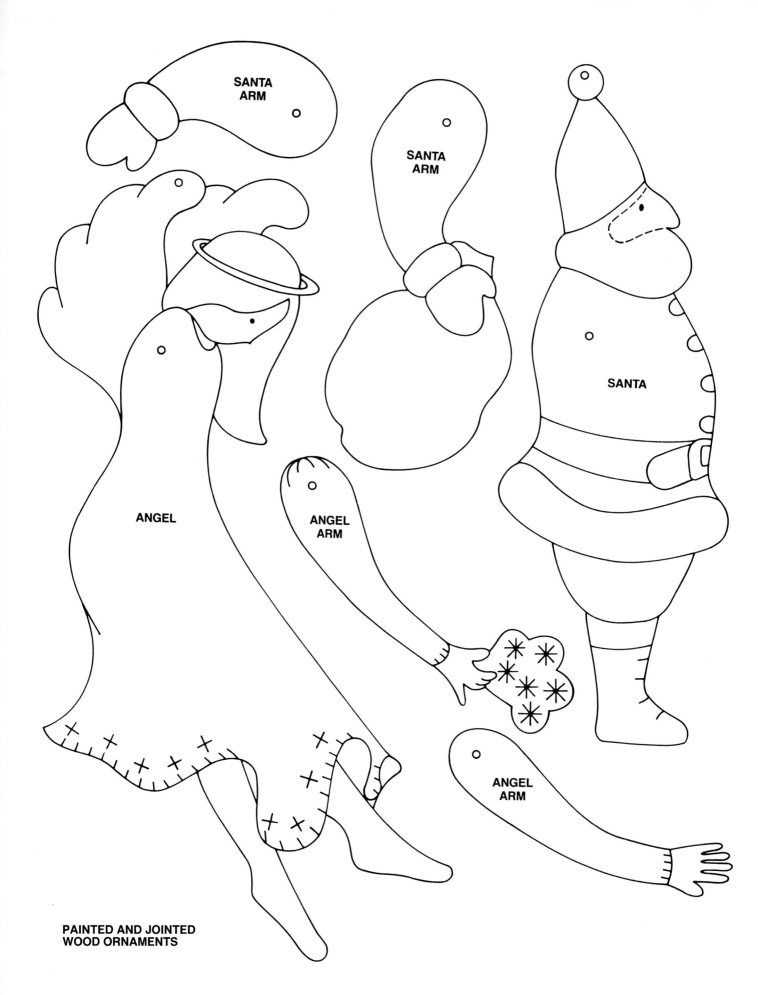

SANTA
ARM

SANTA
ARM

SANTA

ANGEL

ANGEL
ARM

ANGEL
ARM

**PAINTED AND JOINTED
WOOD ORNAMENTS**

Base-paint the red-and-white striped Santa with white paint. Add red stripes on clothing and hat. Paint the bag blue. Paint the face and area between boots with flesh color. The boots, mittens, and eyes are painted black.

Base-paint the red-coat Santa with flesh color. Paint the coat red and the belted tie green. Paint the beard and fur trims white. Add black dots for eyes.

After paint has dried, paint several coats of varnish on Santas.

FINISHING: Drill ⅛-inch holes in tops of ornaments. Thread length of gold cording through each hole for hanging.

PAINTED FOLK-ART SANTAS

ACKNOWLEDGMENTS

We would like to extend our special thanks to the following designers who contributed projects to this book. When more than one project appears on a page, the acknowledgment cites both the project and the page number. A page number alone indicates one designer contributed all of the projects on that page.

Barbara Bennett for Cernit—50–51, easy-bake boy, girl, Santa, and reindeer

Susan Carson—68–69, sweater hearts

Kathy Carter—24–25, tatted snowflakes

Sue Cornelison—40–41, cross-stitch animals

Pam Dyer—4–5, wood ornaments; 8; 18–19, angels and tree topper; 68–69, angels

Linda Emmerson—24–25, cut-paper angel; 71, folk-art Santas

Kathy Engel—71, jointed wood ornaments

Marina Grant—40, wood animals

Sandi Jorgensen and Clara Vujnovich—4–5, candy wreaths; 9

The Karper Collection—4–5 and 6, cat, elephant, and donkey; 25, Victorian Santa

Gail Kinkead—20, crocheted hat, fan, and basket

Mary Sue Kuhn—22, tatted balls

Carol Lisbona—43

Patricia Misgen—42, bear, cat, and bunny

Christine Noah-Cooper—24–25, paper flowers

Deborah Pappenheimer—53

Nancy Reames—4–5, star garland; 7; 18–19, hearts; 20, paper star; 21, topiary; 50–51, cut-paper sheep and elephant; 52; 70

Valerie Root—54–55

Barbara Smith—22, smocked balls

Karen Taylor—68–69, cross-stitch quilt pillows

Ciba Vaughan—23

Judy Veeder—21, bird's nest, bow, and heart; 42, goose

Bonnie Wedge—50–51, cut-paper horse

We also are pleased to acknowledge the following photographers whose talents and technical skills contributed to this book.

Hopkins Associates—40; 43; 71
Scott Little—18–22; 25; 52
Bradley Olman—23
Perry Struse—4–9; 20, small photo; 24–25; 40–42; 50–51; 53–55; 68–70

If you would like to order any additional copies of our books, call 1-800-678-2803 or check with your local bookstore.